Oct. 17, 1972

Highlights

JUMBO

Holiday Handbook

Foreword

From the wealth of materials published in earlier issues of HIGHLIGHTS FOR CHILDREN, we have selected and adapted those features which seem to have the greatest merit in the light of our experiences in the schoolroom, and from our observation of teachers and children. This handbook presents suggestions for creative projects for the leading holidays and seasons of the school year.

—*The Editors*, HIGHLIGHTS FOR CHILDREN

O-ISBN-87 534-551-4

Pumpkin With a Personality

By Evelyn White Minshull

Ever get weary of hacking out the same old pumpkin face year after year—triangle nose and eyes, toothy mouth? When you set him in the window, he might be the one you had last year. Or the year before that.

This October, why not have in your window a pumpkin with a face that has real personality?

The possibilities are unlimited. Best of all, the pumpkin face with a personality requires only a little more time and care and no more skill than his stereotyped brother.

Under A are geometric shapes which can be used as a basis for all of the features. Cut several paper shapes like these. Then cut into them as shown.

B shows suggested shapes for eyes, and C for mouths.

D shows a few nose shapes. But usually it's just as well to use a circle, half-circle, or oval for the nose. Let the other features carry the expression.

How do you want your pumpkin to look? Friendly? Sad? Scary? Whichever you choose, the SHAPE of the pumpkin itself is important. A round or nearly round pumpkin goes well with a sad or sulking face. A short, fat pumpkin takes wider features, so will do best for the wide smile of the happy face.

Wash and dry the pumpkin. Set it on several thicknesses of newspaper on the table or floor. Have ready a sharp paring knife, a large spoon, and a pencil.

With your pencil, sketch a line where the scalp cut should be made. Make sure that this cut is made fairly high, so the features won't be crowded.

Cut off the top of the pumpkin and hollow out the insides, using the large spoon to loosen stubborn areas.

To help you decide on features, here are a few sample faces.

Ever think of eyebrows? Dimples? Even ears? Your pumpkin may need one or all of these to round out his personality.

Notice what a difference the mouth makes. Using the same eyes, nose, and eyebrows, three different mouths produce mirthful, menacing, or mournful faces.

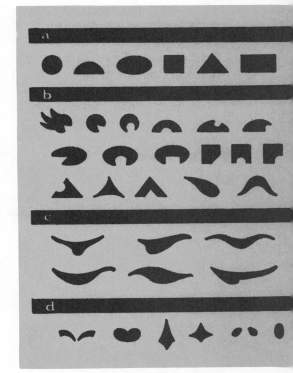

Of course, you can think of lots of different faces.

When you have yours planned, sketch the features on the best side of the pumpkin with the pencil. The lines will be faint, but will prove a great help in your cutting. CAUTION: Before making any cut in the face, make sure that the mouth is not too close to the bottom.

Cut out the features slowly and carefully. Place the candle inside, light it, cap the pumpkin, then sit back and admire your handiwork and your pumpkin face's individual personality.

Happy Witch Decoration

By Ella L. Langenberg

Halloween is the time for fun with witches, skeletons, and the October moon. To make a decoration like the one shown, draw a picture of a witch. To make the witch look happy, draw the corners of her mouth pointing upward.

The figure will look funny with "skeleton ribs." Draw them to look like twisted ribbon, as shown. Cut out the spaces between the loops. Color the dress, hat, and features with black. Leave the face and ribs white.

Cut out the witch and paste it on a large moon made of orange tissue or construction paper. Decorate a window or a wall space with this gay ornament.

Jolly Jack-o'-lantern Baskets

By Agnes V. Ranney

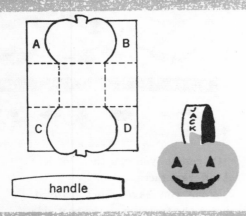

Make the basket pattern shown, on 5-by-7-inch paper. Trace around it on orange construction paper. Cut out on the solid lines. Fold carefully on the dotted lines.

Cut eyes, nose, and mouth from black construction paper, and paste in place on one of the pumpkin shapes.

Fold and paste section A over B, and C over D, with top edges even, to form a square basket. Then paste the pumpkin shapes to the sides of the basket.

Cut the handle from green construction paper. Print the guest's name on it with black crayon. Paste the handle ends back of the pumpkin stems.

Fill with salted nuts, candy corn, and plump raisins.

Toy Totem Pole

By Jacqueline Selzer

Many years ago, Indians liked to carve and paint totem poles, which were their family crests that told stories about their lives. Sometimes these poles were more than fifty feet tall.

Small totem poles can be made out of empty thread spools. Just paint or color a human or animal face on each spool. Then glue the spools together, one on top of the other, as high as they will go. Cut noses, eyes, ears, bills, wings, and feet out of small pieces of paper or cardboard. Glue them to the faces.

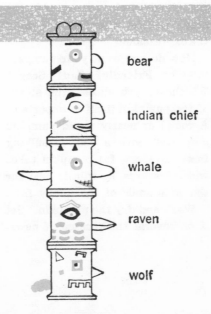

bear

Indian chief

whale

raven

wolf

Let's Draw Beanies

By Valrie M. Geier

Beanies are created with lima beans. Paste them to light-blue or green construction paper so the beans will stand out in bold relief, like 3-D pictures.

Paint a face or body on the bean with black paint or ink. Sketch the rest of the figure on the paper around the bean, using black crayon or charcoal pencil.

The illustrations give ideas to start with. After making a few, try some original ideas. It's fun to make up these odd little figures and animals.

A Book of Pressed Leaves

By Ouida Moore

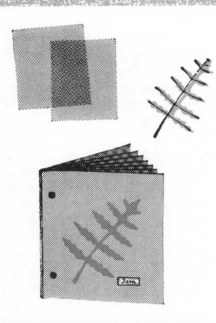

A book may be made of the leaves collected on nature walks; by pressing each leaf between two sheets of waxed paper with a warm iron.

Measure the largest leaf. Cut two pieces of waxed paper about an inch longer and 2 inches wider than the leaf. Count the number of leaves to be put in the book, multiply by two, and cut that many pieces of waxed paper the same size as those cut for the largest leaf. Two or three of the smaller leaves may be arranged on one page. Write the name of each leaf clearly on a small slip of paper and press it between the two pieces of waxed paper, along with the leaves.

Use a warm iron, set for "rayon" or "silk." The heat melts the wax a bit, coats the leaf and preserves its color, and sticks the two pieces of waxed paper together to form a single page.

Each leaf or group of leaves should be arranged slightly to the right of center, so that there is a margin at the left for fastening the pages together to form a book. Two-pronged paper fasteners may be used, or the pages may be stitched together with yarn.

Notebook Covers

By M. Mable Lunz

Buy a package of notebook paper the size wanted. It can be small for the desk or large for school.

Cut the cover twice as wide as the paper, plus 1 inch, and as long as the paper, plus ½ inch. If the paper is larger than four inches, add 1½ inches to the width and ¾ inch to the length.

Fold the cover in half and round off the corners. Punch holes near the folded edge to match those in the paper. Place the paper in the cover and tie together through the holes as shown, with leather or plastic lacing. For large notebooks use metal notebook rings instead of lacing.

To make a heavier cover, cut two pieces of the material the same size. Put the wrong sides together and round off the corners. Punch holes all around, ¼ inch in from the edge and ½ inch apart. If the material is too heavy for a punch, hammer the holes in with a nail.

Lace a strip of leather or plastic through the holes and over the edge as shown. Short pieces of lacing may be joined together with household cement and held with a paper clip until dry.

Punch holes through the folded side of the cover to match those in the paper. Tie cover and paper together with lacing. Use metal rings for large notebooks.

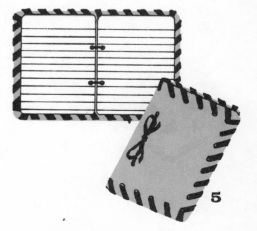

5

Clothespin Fun

By Barbara Baker

With a little imagination and some paint, crayons, colored paper or cloth, and odds and ends for trim, ordinary wooden clothespins can be made into any number of things. Pictured and described here are samples of what can be done. But do try something different. The real fun is in starting with the basic parts, then selecting the material and adding individual ideas from whatever colorful materials are at hand.

Donkey

This is three clothespins stained with brown shoe polish, two of them wired together for body and legs, the third attached upside down for head and ears. The tail is nylon bristles. The circular paper hat is clipped in the center to slip over the ears. The paper eyelashes are fringed for that shy, sleepy look. All other additions are paper, decorated with contrasting paper.

Donkey Head

The ears and face are painted, with fringed paper eyelashes and paper tie added. The hat is a circle of felt with a real feather.

Bird

The body and eyes are painted. The fringed eyelashes and crest are from paper. The feathers are different colors of paper pasted one over the other. The bill is two pieces of toothpick, pushed into a hole in the head of the clothespin.

Clown

The clothespin body is pushed into two clay feet, painted to look like shoes. The arms are a piece of pipe cleaner twisted around the head of the clothespin and bent to shape, with ends inserted between paper hand shapes. The ruff is crepe paper pleated on wire and fastened around the neck. The head is a small, used flashbulb with sequin eyes, big bead nose, and yarn hair. The hat is a cone of colored paper topped with a real feather. The rest of the decoration is confetti.

Pumpkin-face Favors

By Evelyn W. Minshull

The "pumpkin" at the left is an orange. A short piece of pipe cleaner is the stem. Paint the features with ink, or a black felt-tipped marker.

The one at the right is a marshmallow. Using food coloring and a toothpick "brush," paint the features on one of the flat sides. Break off the end of the toothpick and use it as a matching stem.

Witch Pin   By Barbara Baker

Cut and paste together a 2½-inch black felt circle, and a smaller yellow one, with cardboard circle between. Make the broom from a twig with grasses wired on the end.

Cut out the black witch. Paste to the yellow circle with the broom between.   Add a half-sequin eye. Sew a small safety pin on the back of the pin.

Paper Bag Funny Doll

By Ruth Libbey

Six paper bags are needed—a small one for the head, four larger ones for the arms and legs, and one the same size or a little larger for the body. Color a funny face on the head. Stuff torn paper in the head and body.

Split the body bag as shown. Tie on the legs with colored yarn. Put the head into the other end of the body. Tie with yarn.

With a large needle and yarn, sew the arms to the body. Tie yarn around the wrists.

Circus Wagons   By Evelyn Walker

Cut two strips of red poster paper, ¾ by 6 inches. Cut two strips 1 by 6 inches. Cut four circles for wheels. Cut twenty strips of black paper, ¼ by 4½ inches, for bars on cages. Draw and cut out two animals from tan paper.

Assemble the two circus wagons on a large sheet of poster paper. Paste on animals first. Place the black strips over the animals, and paste the ends of the strips only.

Cover these, top and bottom, with the red strips. Paste on the wheels. Join the wagons with tongues of red paper, as shown.

Quick-and-easy Indian Headdress   By Virginia Appelt

Cut a strip of corrugated cardboard 1 to 2 inches wide and long enough to go around the head. Fasten the ends of the strip together with cellophane tape or attach a piece of string to each end to tie on the headdress.

Stick the feathers down into the ridges of the corrugated cardboard all around, or place a few together at one side. The feathers can always be rearranged.

7

Pie Faces

By M. Mable Lunz

Each face is an aluminum foil pan such as frozen pie comes in. The pan is cut to the shape of face desired.

Anything that is added to the face must be made with extra tabs or ends. These can be pushed through holes in the face and folded in back, to hold the feature in place.

Noses

Cut different sizes and shapes from a foil pan. Bend at the center. Bend the sides in.

Mustache

Cut from foil pan.

Eyes

Shape from blue or black pipe cleaner.

Mouths

Shape from two pieces of red pipe cleaner.

Moon Face

Cut a pan in half. Cut strips from the center to a 1-inch rim. Fold strips back over the rim. Fasten the rim to the foil plate. Add the other features.

Curly Head

Cut strips in the top edge for curls. Cut off the rim area for the chin shape. Curl the strips forward over the face by rolling them over the end of pencil or water color brush. Cut a half pan as for Moon Face. Curl the strips back over the rim. Fasten the rim under the first curls. Add the other features.

Bearded Man

Cut away the rim areas. Cut strips as shown for hair and beard. Curl the beard strips. Use another half pan to make a longer beard. Add other features.

Halloween Candy Man

By Ella L. Langenberg

Cover a cylinder-shaped cereal box with orange paper. Cut black paper eyes, nose, mouth, and eyebrows. Paste them in place. Paste on a white paper tooth, and white crescent shapes on the eyes as shown. Make the necktie from ribbon or a strip of paper. Paste in place.

Glue or sew an aluminum foil pie plate to the top of the box. Fill it with candies.

A Candy Man of this size will make a nice centerpiece to decorate the table.

Individual place favors may be made from smaller containers such as frozen fruit juice comes in. For this size use a crinkled paper baking cup at the top to hold the candy.

Halloween Window Decorations

By Betsy Ann Page

Use a clear plastic spool from a cellophane tape refill for the foundation of each decoration.

From orange construction paper cut two jack-o'-lanterns to fit the spool. Cut out the features. Paste green tissue paper to the back of each lantern. Trim the edges. Paste one lantern on each side of the spool, matching the features so the light will shine through.

Use a piece of black thread for a hanger.

Make a black cat's head. Use white thread for whiskers.

Cut out a witch's face from white construction paper. Add a black hat.

These are suggestions. Now make some original decorations.

Indian Fun

By Mabel L. Sansing

A man's old shirt can be made into an Indian costume. Cut off the collar, then cut off the sleeves to fit. Fringe the ends of the sleeves and around the bottom of the shirt.

Punch holes along the side seams, through both front and back. Cut holes around the neck. Thread black or brown yarn through the holes, and tie.

Draw Indian designs around the bottom, on the sleeves, and on the front and back. Color them with crayons, and press with a warm iron.

A feather held in place with a ribbon, some old costume jewelry, and a little lipstick war paint complete the costume.

Clown Place Card

By Luella Pierce

Cut a round ice-cream carton lid in half. On white paper draw a clown face large enough to fit into the half lid. Color the clown's face, cap, and ruff, and paste it to the inside of the lid. Write the guest's name on the clown's cap. Make one for each guest. These can also be used for the tray of a shut-in or hospital patient.

A small nut cup filled with tiny goodies may be glued to or just placed under the clown's chin. The little clown face will rock back and forth.

A Cork Horse

By Margaret Whittemore

A good-sized cork makes the body. A smaller cork makes the head. Toothpicks will serve for legs. The mane and tail are black wool. The ears are bits of brown paper. The eyes are black-headed pins.

Fasten the paper saddle and stirrups in place with gummed tape, running it around the horse's body for a girth.

Box Heads

By Lillie D. Chaffin

Make strange Halloween faces from small cardboard boxes.

Cut an inch or two from three sides of the box. Shape the bottom of the fourth side to resemble a chin.

Use colored paper or cloth to make hair and eyebrows. Cut holes for the eyes and nose. The teeth, lips, and ears may be drawn on the box, or they may be cut and pasted on. Jack-o'-lantern earrings may be tied on with string. Horns, paper hats, and other items may be added to the box heads.

For fun at a Halloween party, give each guest a box and have scissors, paper, and crayons handy. Give a prize for the prettiest, and one for the strangest box head.

Autumn Harvest Scene

By Agnes Choate Wonson

On a panel of white construction paper paint a water-color sky above a brown cornfield, with violet trees along the horizon. Dot in corn stubbles with brown crayon.

The rest of the scenery is pasted on. Fence posts are black braid or elastic with black wool rails. Corn shocks are 2-inch lengths of brown wool tied together at the top. The scarecrow is cut from felt, the crows are black yarn, and the clouds are white cotton. Pumpkins are small orange buttons with green wool vines.

Jointed Pumpkin Man

By Betsy Ann Page

From orange construction paper cut the head, body, arms, and legs as shown. Cut the slots indicated. Slip the arms and legs through the proper slots and fasten in back with a two-pronged paper fastener. Pull the head and the pumpkin man will move his arms and legs.

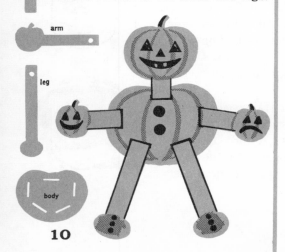

10

Halloween Costume

By Ruth Libbey

Use a large paper bag such as is used for suits from the cleaner's. Do **not** use plastic ones.

If you haven't such a bag, use a long piece of wide wrapping paper. Fold it in half. The fold is the shoulder line. Cut out the neck, and slit down the middle front about 8 inches. Tape the sides together under the armholes. Cut some slits at the bottom so the skirt part will not tear.

Draw and color a big pumpkin on each side of the costume—perhaps a smiling one on one side and a scowly one on the other side. Draw and color some autumn leaves here and there to make it more festive.

Real colored autumn leaves make a pretty wreath to wear. Or draw and color some out of stiff paper.

Scarecrow Costume

By Sylvia Sanders

Use an old, worn, oversize shirt, and trousers or slacks. Straw, hay, cornhusks, shredded paper, or the like, is sewed to the bottoms of the sleeves and pants.

Slide a broom handle through both sleeves. Hold the pole in place inside the shirt at the shoulders with small loops made of bias tape. Then tie the edges of the sleeves to the pole with rope or twine. When the costume is worn, the arms are not put into the shirt sleeves, though they appear to be.

After slipping into the trousers, tie separate ropes around each ankle. An old battered hat, with wisps of stuffing sticking out from under, completes the costume.

A paper-bag mask is very appropriate and simple for a face covering. An even safer and more comfortable suggestion would be a scarecrow face created with stage make-up, usually available at a drugstore.

Corni

By Bess Lintner

Pull back the cornhusks and remove the silk. Wrap a 7-inch wire around the corn body, about two-thirds of the way down, twisting the wires to within 2½ inches from the ends. Twist another wire in the same way with the ends on the opposite side. Cover the four ends with pipe cleaner. Bend them so the corn body will stand.

Cut off the husks to the shape shown, fastening them in back with gummed tape. Add a headband of pipe cleaners, twisting in back and spreading the ends. Tape on paper reinforcement-ring eyes, a gummed-star nose, and pipe-cleaner mouth and arms. Tape on a colored crepe paper skirt trimmed with gummed stars, pieces of cornhusks, and bits of paper ribbon. Add a pipe-cleaner belt. Use colored pipe cleaners, or color them later—the more colors, the better.

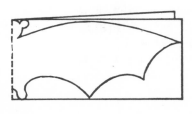

Owl Candy Box

By Agnes Choate Wonson

On heavy gray construction paper, draw the pattern shown. Cut it out. Use reinforcement circles for eyes. Add eye pupils and feathers with black crayon. Color the beaks yellow.

Cut out the bottom of the beaks BELOW the dotted line ONLY. Fold the heads along the dotted lines. Fasten the corners together inside the box with gummed tape. The four yellow beaks form legs for the box to stand on. Fill it with candy corn.

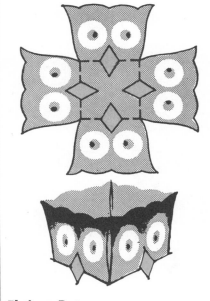

Flying Bat

By Bea Blasing

On a fold of black construction paper, draw and cut out half a bat shape. To the wing tips fasten black elastic such as comes on Halloween masks. Tie a thread handle to the rubber and bounce the bat to make it "fly."

Gumdrop Animals

By Evelyn White Minshull

These cute and clever animals are made from two sizes of gumdrops, colored pipe cleaners, and toothpicks. They can be made all one color, or mixed colors.

The head is one large gumdrop with the flat part at the back. The body is two large ones with the flat sides down. The legs are made from small gumdrops, the number used depending on the length of legs needed. The deer is made like the bunny, with longer legs and no whiskers.

Assemble each body with toothpicks. Finish the head before sticking it onto the body with half a toothpick. Curve short pieces of pipe cleaner and insert for eyes. Stick a tiny piece straight in for a nose. Shape ears as needed, and cut whiskers about an inch long. Stick them in until firm. Use a small gumdrop for the bunny's tail, and a shaped pipe cleaner for the cat's tail.

The bunny's body, with a bushy feather tail and smaller pointed ears, would become a fox. The cat, with the same bushy tail, would become a squirrel. A camel would need a neck, but the humps would be easy. A bird could have toothpick legs and gumdrop feet.

Try a lamb, lion, puppy, or cow. There's no end to the creatures you can make with gumdrops.

11

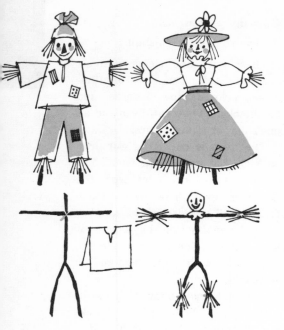

Halloween Scarecrows   By Ella L. Langenberg

Find a forked stick that will make the legs and body. If the scarecrow is to be used for outdoor decoration, the stick should be strong enough to stand up when pushed into the ground. For a table decoration, push a forked stick, 10 or 12 inches high, into a mound of clay. Tie a second stick across the first one to make the arms.

Make a ball of cotton for the head. Cover it with flesh-colored plastic or a nylon stocking. Pull it down, and tie it around the neck. Color the features with ink or paint.

Sew grass, cornhusks, or raffia to the head. Tie some at the wrists and ankles.

Tie or sew pieces of cloth on the arms and legs. Pad the body with cotton or cloth to give it shape, if desired.

Cut a shirt or blouse like the pattern shown. For the girl's skirt, gather a piece of cloth and sew in place. Cut her hat from felt with a hole at the top, so it will pull down on the head. The boy's cap is a piece of sock, gathered at the top.

One-leaf Pictures

By Bernice Walz

Select any kind of leaf. Paste it in the center of a piece of construction paper. Use the leaf for the body. With crayons, add heads, legs, and tails to make pictures of all kinds of animals. Try making people, too. See how many different pictures can be made.

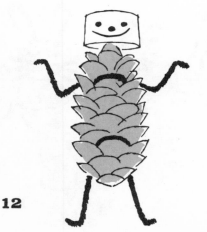

Halloween Hobgoblin   By Carolyn F. Young

Each hobgoblin requires one long, narrow pine cone, two colored pipe cleaners, and a large marshmallow. Bend the pipe cleaners around the cone, one near the top and one near the stem end, as shown. Twist them at the back, bring them out the sides, and bend them into arm and leg shapes.

With a soft lead pencil draw eyes, nose, and mouth on the round side of the marshmallow. Press it firmly down over the top of the cone, as shown.

Use them for party favors or for the dinner table.

Owlet
By Hilda K. Watkins

For the body, wrap cotton around a small bottle with a narrow neck.

Make the head and wings from a square of brown paper as shown. Cut in from the corners on the straight lines. Fold the points forward on the dotted lines. Paste them together, but not to the back of the head. Cut slits in the wings and tail for feathers. Slip the head down over the neck of the bottle.

Paint brown feathers on the cotton breast and other parts of the body. Add black eyes and beak.

  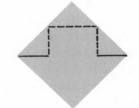 

A Witch for Halloween
By Frances Benson

Wrap a double strip of yellow or orange crepe paper around a broom. Glue it securely.

From black paper, cut big eyes and eyebrows, a nose, and a mouth with big teeth (some of them missing). Paste these on the crepe paper to make the witch's face.

Cut some short lengths of rope. Shred them into strings. Fasten to the broomstraws for hair.

From black crepe paper, make a hat and a cape for the witch. Gather the cape around the broom handle immediately beneath the witch's face, and tie it tightly with string.

Surprise your friends by holding the broom up at a window where they will be sure to see it.

Crepe-paper Bug
By Katherine Corliss Bartow

Wrap a 2½-by-8-inch piece of colored crepe paper around a pencil or dowel, and glue. Let it dry. Draw the design with colored and black crayon on the paper. Push the ends of the paper toward the center of the pencil to crush. Remove from the pencil.

An inch from one end, tie off the head section with thread. Stuff a small ball of tissue in this part for the head. Fold over both ends of the paper, and glue.

Glue on sequin eyes. Antennas are fine wire stuck into head with a bit of glue.

Cut a strip of lightweight cardboard ⅜ inch wide, and as long as the bug from neck to tail. Cut another the same size from paper. Color both. Punch five holes along each side of the cardboard for legs. Cut ten ¾-inch pipe-cleaner legs. Bend one end for feet. Dab glue on the other end and just barely insert through the holes so they do not stick up. Glue a strip of paper over the top of the cardboard. Glue the bug to the paper.

Legs may also be cut out from both sides of a wider cardboard strip, and bent down.

For a glitter bug, glue sequins over the body.

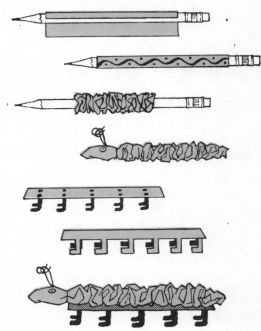

Halloween Witchcraft

By Margaret O. Hyde

Strange things can happen on Halloween. Here are some ways to prove that the witches are at work.

The Witch's Candle

Clean a piece of glass and stand it upright by piling books on each side of it.

Place a burning candle in front of the glass, and a tumbler of water at the same distance behind the glass.

Look through the glass and you will see the witch's candle burning in the water.

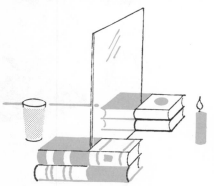

Witch's Brew

Wash an empty soda bottle and put two tablespoonfuls of ink into it. Fill the bottle with hot water.

Wash another soda bottle and fill it with cold water.

Be sure that both bottles are filled to the very top.

Cover the cold-water bottle with a tiny square of heavy paper and press down hard on the paper with your thumb.

Holding the paper square in place, set the cold-water bottle, mouth down, on top of the bottle with hot ink in it. Carefully slide out the paper square, holding the top bottle in place.

Watch the blue ink rise to make Witch's Brew.

Look at the Ghost

Make a big black ghost on a large sheet of paper. Leave white spaces for mouth, eyes, and nose. Hang the paper on the wall, or prop it upright on a table.

Ask friends to stare at the white mouth of the ghost for one minute while you time them. Then ask them to look at a white surface for another minute. A sheet, the ceiling, or a white wall are good places to look. They will see a big white ghost appear and disappear.

Mystery Pumpkin Game
By Maude D. Baltzell

Prepare the pumpkins ahead of time, one for each guest. Cut them from yellow or orange construction paper. Write a number on the back of half of them, then copy the same numbers on the backs of the other half. Use small numbers so they can easily be totaled. Place all the pumpkins, number side down, in a box.

Two "choosers" select, in turn, the members for their team. These choosers also act as scorekeepers for their team.

A blindfolded player from each team selects a pumpkin. The number on the pumpkin is written on a score card for his team. When all players have had a turn, the team with the highest total count wins the game.

Table-top Circus

By Bernice Walz

Circus Clown

Punch a hole in the center of 26 bottle caps, using hammer and nail. From foil or other paper, cut circles larger than the cap. Cover each cap, folding the edges inside. The foil will stay in place. Use rubber cement to hold the other paper.

For each leg, run a 6-inch pipe cleaner through seven bottle caps, alternating colors. Push the caps to the bottom of the cleaner. Fold end to hold caps. Bring the two cleaners together to make the waist. Run the two cleaners through five caps for the body; through a hole in the cork for the head; then through a covered cap, hollow-side up, for the hat. Twist the ends around an artificial flower. Paste bits of colored paper for eyes, nose, and mouth. Cement curly metallic pieces for hair.

For arms, put three caps on either end of a 6-inch pipe cleaner. Reverse last cap to finish the sleeve. Fold over ends for hands. Twist center around neck. Add ribbon necktie.

Make the umbrella by pushing a 6-inch pipe cleaner through a covered cap, folding the end. Hook the other end to the clown's hand. Let the umbrella touch the floor to help the clown to stand.

Midget Acrobats

Fold a 6-inch pipe cleaner in half. Push looped end through the center of a covered cap for the skirt, then into a small marshmallow for the head. The bottle cap could be lined with a circle from a lace-paper doily to make a larger skirt. Make eyes, nose and mouth with colored ink. Cement metallic curls for hair. Use small cake decoration for hair trim. Twist a cleaner around neck for arms. Cut to the right length, and bend ends to make hands.

Make several acrobats, using different colors for the skirts. Stick the feet of one acrobat into a large gumdrop. Place in circus ring. Another can ride on the back of any small toy animal. Balance another on the ring by sticking her feet into one of the corrugated sections.

Trapeze

Push two red-and-white candy sticks into large marshmallows to make them stand. Make a bar by twisting the ends of a 12-inch pipe cleaner around the tops of the candy sticks. Fasten a pipe-cleaner trapeze to the bar. Put an acrobat on it.

Animals

Make a horse, lion, tiger, and other animals. Twist the centers of two pipe cleaners together for the body, bending the four ends for legs. Twist on extra pipe cleaners for body, head, and tail. Use metallic curls for mane and tail; small pieces of marshmallows for feet.

Make the turtle from a bottle cap covered with green metallic paper. Cut three short pieces of green pipe cleaner. Twist together at the center. Press the center into the cap. Hold in place with metallic paper. Spread and shape the six ends—four legs, a tail, and neck. Stick a bit of marshmallow on the neck for a head.

Circus Ring

Cut a strip of corrugated paper ½ inch wide and about 40 inches long. Several strips can be fastened together to get the length. Place the ring on a large circle of brown wrapping paper. Fill with sawdust.

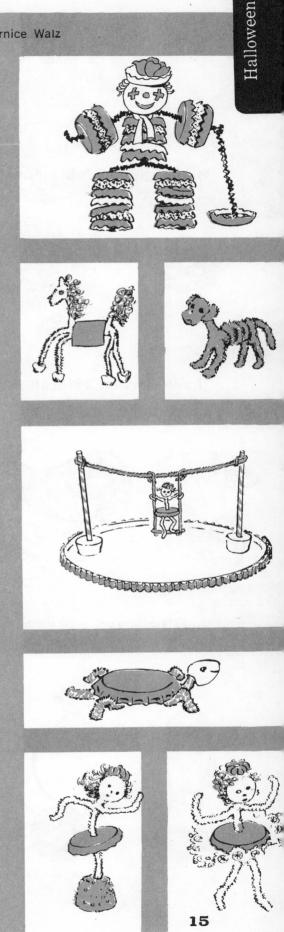

15

Things To Do

Thanksgiving Table Favor

By Ruth Dougherty

Insert two toothpicks into a prune to form the turkey's legs and body. Break off a small portion from another toothpick, and stick it in at the tail. Spear six raisins onto the rest of the toothpick for the neck. Top the raisin neck with a small marshmallow to make the head. Tie on a small length of red yarn to represent the wattle.

Push the center of a paper candy cup over the toothpick tail to make the feathers. Stick the toothpick legs into a large colored gumdrop, so the turkey will stand.

Thanksgiving Decoration

By Ella L. Langenberg

An appropriate decoration for Thanksgiving is a fruit-filled cornucopia, also called a "horn of plenty." The word cornucopia means plenty or abundance.

Draw a horn on 9-by-12-inch white construction paper. Color it yellow, orange, and brown. Cut slits as shown.

Draw and color fruit. At the bottom or side of each piece, draw a tab as shown. Cut out the fruit. Fold back the tabs and push them through the slits in the horn. Paste the tabs to the underside of the horn, and the fruit will stand away from it.

Novelty Pins

By Barbara Baker

Prudence is made from a small ice-cream spoon. Fasten a small safety pin to the back with gummed tape, running it through the pin and around the spoon to secure it. The features and hair are sequins. The dress is crepe paper, the arms a strip of matching paper. The hands and apron are bits of white paper doily. The shoes are black paper with round sequins cut square. The bonnet is bell-shaped white paper with a slit across the top to slide over the head.

The turkey is a cork ball with colored toothpick feathers. The neck is a short toothpick with a bead head stuck on the end. The nose and comb are bits of red felt. The eyes are sequins. The legs are pins with sequins and beads strung on them. The wing is colored felt. Put a small safety pin on one end of a ribbon or string. Pin the other end to the cork.

16

Oscar, the Owl

By Luella Pierce

Fold 9-by-12-inch construction paper to 6-by-9 size. Draw the body with the top part on the fold. Cut it out, leaving the fold uncut. Using yellow construction paper about 5½ inches square, draw and cut out the head. For the feathers, cut white paper like the lower part of the head. Slash it about an inch deep and paste in place. With colored crayons, draw the face, wings, and other lines.

Fasten the head to the top center of the body with a two-prong paper fastener. The head will turn from side to side. The feet can be spread so the owl will stand.

Cabin Picture

By Barbara Baker

Choose a piece of thin board or heavy cardboard the size the picture is to be. Gather together twigs, small leaves and weeds, pine needles, small stones, burned matchsticks, bark, and the like.

With paint or water colors, put in the sky and ground, and a lake if desired. Use burned matches for trunks of small trees. Stain them for the cabin. Bark will make the trunks of the larger trees. Use small stones for the chimney; and leaves, weeds, and pine needles for the foliage. After the parts have been placed as desired, glue them to the board.

Rhythm Shaker and Cymbals

By Evelyn Walker

Force a small paper cup, bottom end first, into the end of a paper-towel tube. Put in a few beans, then force another paper cup into the tube, open end first, to completely block the tube opening. Cut a strip of crepe paper 18 by 6 inches. Fringe it as shown. Wrap the uncut edge around the end of the tube and paste on, letting the fringe dangle. Cover the entire tube with construction paper.

For the cymbals, use a tin lid with a lip, the kind that snaps in or screws on, to avoid sharp edges. Nail a 1-inch piece of broomstick to the center of the lid for the handle. A pair of these make very good rhythm cymbals, not too loud.

Greeting-card Bookmarks

By Ouida Johnston Moore

Look at old greeting cards for the prettiest or most interesting parts. Place a drinking glass on a card, carefully centering the part to be used. Draw around the edge, and cut out the circle. Do the same for the second part you want to use. Place the circles back to back. Cut a matching or harmonizing ribbon 12 to 15 inches long. Fold it in half, put the fold between the two circles, and paste together. Be sure to put paste all around the inside edge of the circles and a dab in the center to hold the ribbon in place. Press the circles together firmly with the ribbon between.

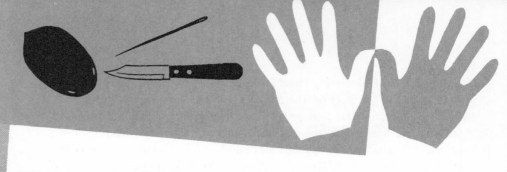

Little Pecan-head Dolls   By Texie Hering

Use pecan nuts in the shell for doll heads. At one end of the nut, bore a hole on either side, as shown, using a sharp knife point. Or ask Mother to make the holes for you. Push a large needle through the holes from side to side, to pierce the kernel.

Use a pipe cleaner for each body side, one third for an arm and two thirds for a leg. Push the shorter part through the holes in the head. Bring the ends down under the head, and twist. Do the same for the other arm and leg, twisting around the top of the first section. Twist legs across each other, about an inch down from the head. This forms the body.

Use quick-drying black paint for hair. Or cut a 1-inch circle of black crepe paper, slash the edge, and glue on for hair. Or bits of black yarn may be used. Using quick-drying paint, make white-circle eyes or slanted oriental eyes with black centers; also a white mouth and white dots for the nose.

Make a whole family—mother, father, son, and daughter—and dress them, using strips of colored crepe paper, fastening ends with gummed tape. Or cut double folds of crepe paper, fasten under the arms and inside the legs. Bend the dolls to sit down or to dance gaily. The body may also be wound with brown paper strips to match the head.

Totem Pole and Caterpillar   By Agnes Woodward

One egg carton will make two caterpillars. Cut the carton in half. Paint the two halves with bright colors. Insert pipe-cleaner antennae in the heads as shown. Paste on white circles for eyes, with black paint centers.

The totem pole is made from one whole egg carton. Wire on maca-roni arms. Paste on paper circle eyes or paint them on. Paste on wings cut from silver paper. Add other bits of decoration such as buttons and pieces of pipe cleaner. The carton may be painted first, or the paint may be added last, working a color scheme around the oth-er decorations.

Bookworm Bookmark   By Geneva Halladay

From heavy colored or figured paper, cut circles, starting with one about 1¼ inches wide for the head. For the body, cut two circles a little smaller than the head, then three a little smaller than that, then three still smaller. Three more tiny circles form both the tail end and the feet.

Overlap the circles to form the worm, then paste them together. A tiny dot of paste is plenty for each part. A hump in the body lets the worm curl over the top of the page.

Draw on the mouth, and paste on sequin eyes.

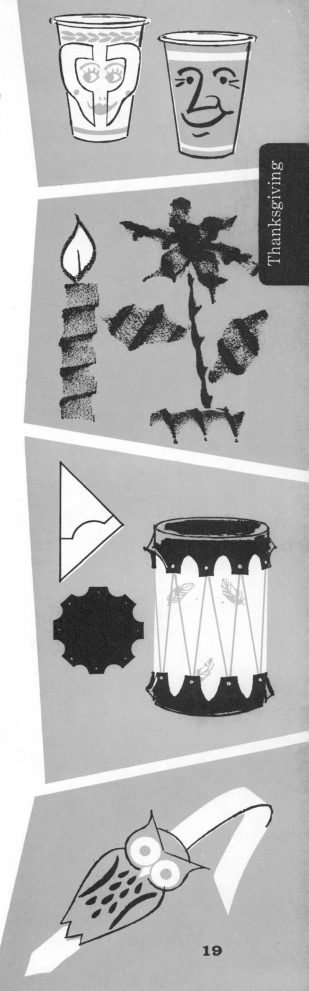

Paper Cup People   By Evelyn White Minshull

For a clever touch when entertaining, try paper cup people. Be sure to place the decorations well down from the cup edge so the mouth won't touch the ink or paint.

With felt-tipped markers, draw faces on the paper cups in which the beverage will be served. Several colors may be used on white cups. But if the cups are colored ones, it's best to use black for all the features. If the cups have a decorative edge around the top, this could serve as the hairline. If the cups have handles, the face has ready-made ears.

Drawing With Corrugated Paper   By Luella Pierce

Place newsprint over corrugated paper. Run colored crayons lightly back and forth over the newsprint. Turn the paper different ways to get different effects. Experiment with different combinations of colors. Light colors, with darker colors run over them lightly, will give an iridescent effect.

Many interesting designs may be made, as well as trees, flowers, and other pictures.

Indian Drum   By Tera Burgundy

This drum is made from scraps from an old rubber inner tube, and a five-quart oil can. These can be found at almost any service station.

Turn the can upside down to drain out the excess oil. Cut out the top and bottom, using a can opener. Place the can in hot soapy water and scrub clean. Rinse with clear water.

When dry, paint can with white enamel or any suitable paint on hand. Apply two or more coats. Let dry thoroughly.

Fold a 12-inch square of newspaper in half twice. Fold again to form a triangle. Draw a line ½ inch long from the fold on both sides, 5½ inches from the top. Draw a curve between the two lines as shown. Keep the newspaper folded, and cut along this line with scissors. Unfold the pattern.

Slit the inner tube open. Clean with a damp cloth, and place inside out on a flat surface. Place the pattern on it and trace around it with chalk. Cut it out with scissors. Cut out two of these. Punch a hole about ¾ inch in from each of the straight edges.

Place one piece over the can bottom, and one over the top. Using leather or plastic thong or twine, lace the two pieces together as shown. Pull the ends tightly in place, and tie with a hard knot.

Stick feathers around to decorate the drum, or paint on Indian signs if desired.

Owl Bookmark   By Thelma T. Royer

Make a paper pattern of the owl and cut the shape out of brown or black felt or construction paper. Add a little triangle of yellow for the beak.

If felt is used, sew on two white buttons for eyes. If paper, use gummed reinforcement rings.

Draw wings and other lines with contrasting color ink. Glue or sew the owl to a piece of yellow ribbon as shown.

Apple-head Dolls
By Agnes Woodward

To make an apple-head doll, you will need a large firm apple, a small paring knife, the empty cylinder from wax paper or paper towels, fine copper wire, cotton batting, water paints, and scrap materials.

Peel the apple, and select the best side for the face. Make hollows a quarter inch deep for eyes and mouth. Shape the nose by carving some of the apple from each side of the nose area.

Paint the eyes and mouth with white paint, and let dry. Then apply the desired eye color, and a red mouth. Use very pale pink on the cheeks and rub it in.

Place the apple in a warm place. Let it dehydrate for several days.

Use a short piece of wire to make eyeglasses, and attach to the nose. Add cotton-batting hair.

Cut the cylinder into sections to be used as bases for the apple heads. The base may be painted to represent clothing, or material may be pasted on.

Use a part of the cylinder for a man's hat. From stiff cardboard, cut out a circle about a quarter of an inch larger than the diameter of the cylinder. Place the cylinder in the center of the circle, and draw around it. Cut out this inner section. Cover the cylinder crown and the cardboard brim with felt or material. Slip the brim over the crown, and attach the hat to the apple head.

Women's hats or bonnets may be made from felt or material with decorations added.

These apple heads are fun to make and will last for years. The older and drier they become, the more they resemble little people.

Light-bulb Creatures
By Agnes Woodward

By using some imagination, all sorts of odd-looking creatures can be created from burned-out light bulbs.

Paint, cotton, dried vegetables, and odds and ends of materials make the features. For example, a cone of painted paper becomes a bird's beak, split peas can be used for eyes, and wild rice grains for eyelashes.

Paper coffee or ice-cream cups make ideal bases, which can be decorated to fit the creation.

Husky Hobgoblin Card
By Agnes Choate Wonson

Cut the body and arms freehand from a dry cornhusk. Paste them on a 3½-by-8-inch piece of black construction paper.

The face is a circle of orange construction paper with black ink features. Add a green hobgoblin cap.

Print a greeting with white ink.

20

Papier-mâché Wall Masks
By Roberta Edelman

The mask is built on the back of a paper plate of the desired size. Punch two tiny holes a little below the rim. Insert string through the holes for a hanger.

Tear newspaper into 1-by-8-inch strips. Soak several strips at a time in a bowl of water until they become limp. Then soak a few strips at a time in a thin paste of flour and water. Apply them to the plate to form a foundation. Add strips until the foundation is about a half-inch thick.

Build up the desired facial features on this foundation. Full, round cheeks or a prominent nose are made by applying many layers of paper strips and molding them into shape.

To form features that project out of the mask such as ears, tongue, eyelashes, cut the shapes from cardboard, cover with small strips of newspaper, and insert in the mask. Cover connecting lines with more strips of newspaper.

When the molding of the mask is finished, add a final layer of strips. Keeping the surface wet, smooth the rough edges with your fingers. Add other decorative features.

Allow the mask to dry for several days until stiff and hard. Don't attempt to lift it by the string until completely dry. Then trim the ragged edges of the plate, and paint the mask as desired.

These masks can be used as wall decorations. Use your imagination to create funny clowns, scary faces, or animals. Or try a self-portrait, or a mask to represent each member of the family.

Nutshell Creatures
By Ruth Dougherty

Save empty shells from different kinds of nuts, and use them to make all sorts of creatures.

Bunnies

Walnut-shell halves make the father and mother, and pistachio shells are used for the babies.

Paint the shells white. When dry, apply a coat of colorless nail polish for protection. If the pistachio shells are red, put on a coat of clear polish before and after painting them white.

Use a toothpick to apply glue to pink bead eyes. A length of white thread, folded into six strands an inch long and tied in a knot in the center, makes the whiskers. Glue in place. Cut ears and teeth from white paper, as illustrated. Color the inside of the ears pink, and glue to the shell. Add a ball of fluffy cotton for a tail.

Set the bunny family in a nest of green-paper grass.

Mice

The mice are made in the same manner as the bunnies, except that they are gray with black bead eyes. The tail is a short length of gray wool yarn. Ears for the baby mice are tiny squares of pink paper rounded slightly at the top. Ears for mother and father mouse are illustrated.

Ladybird Beetles

Paint the walnut-shell halves a dark orange or red, with black spots. A small colored rubber band cut in half is the antennae. Hold in place until dry so it will remain standing.

The baby bugs are dried split peas painted to match mother and father beetle. Glue the baby bugs to a length of thread and fasten to a parent so they won't get lost.

Pilgrim Project

Indians, Pilgrims, and Turkey   By Barbara Baker

The bodies of the Indian and Pilgrims are colored construction paper, rolled into a tube and pasted or stapled together. The arms are a strip of paper, fastened at the back, brought forward, and bent into shape. The hair, facial features, clothing, feet, and trim are also cut from paper and fastened in place.

For the turkey, paste or staple a construction paper tube together at the top. Scallop it as shown. Use several colors of paper for the tail feathers. Staple them to a paper circle, then to the turkey's back.

Some ideas are shown here, but the fun is in trying out original ideas to get the desired effect.

Paper-plate Turkey   By Barbara Baker

Cut a 6-inch circle from colored construction paper. Cut ½-inch slits around the edge, about an inch apart. Bend the cut sections forward. Slit the circle from edge to center, and fold to a cone shape. Place in center of a paper plate. Fasten by the cut sections.

For the head, fold a piece of colored paper over the end of a colored toothpick, and cut to head shape. Cut and paste on a beak of the same color. Add a red wattle. Paint on the eyes. Stick toothpick end into the point of the cone-shaped body.

Insert two more toothpicks for legs. Cut off the paper plate at the bottom as shown, so the turkey will stand. Make slits around the rest of the plate from the edge to the body. Paint the strips in bright colors. Paint wings and feather shapes on the body.

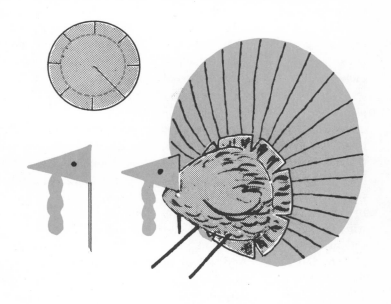

The doll is made from a piece of pink crepe paper, about 4 by 5 inches. Cut three slits as shown by the heavy lines on the diagram.

Roll a small wad of paper, fold the head section over it, and twist two or three times at the neck. Twist the arm and leg sections. Tie them with thread at the wrists and ankles. Make facial features with ink or water colors.

For dresses and suits, fold cloth or crepe paper and cut out like the pattern shown, with the fold on the dotted line. For trouser legs, make a slit up the middle of the skirt section.

For hair, use thread, yarn, or cotton. For other trim, use colored paper, cloth, ribbon, paper doilies, metallic paper, and the like.

Make a miniature collection, sewing the dolls to heavy colored paper. Or use them as favors, varying the colors and trimming to suit the occasion.

A pretty picture can be made with dried flowers, weeds, and grasses found in the garden, on vacant lots, or at the park. Pick flowers or weeds that are pretty, or have interesting shapes. Choose ones that do not crumble.

Paint them with enamel or lacquer to make them more colorful and to preserve them better. When they are dry, place them in a pleasing arrangement on construction paper or cardboard. Mark where each is placed. Apply white glue to the back of each. Press it down firmly on the paper, and wipe off excess glue. Attach a hanger.

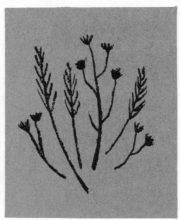

23

An Indian Collar

By Ella L. Langenberg

Clothing worn by Indians long ago was made from animal skins, called buckskin. Indians did not have pretty colored cloth. Neither did they have buttons or zippers, so much of their clothing was made to slip over the head, or to be tied on. Where our clothes are hemmed to make a finish, theirs was slashed to make a decorative fringe. For other trim, they sewed on beads or painted on designs.

Many of these designs were used in Indian picture writing. They did not have a written language like ours. When they wanted to write about the sun, moon, lightning, rivers, mountains, or other things, they drew pictures.

The Indian collar shown is easy to make. Later, other garments could be made, even a complete Indian costume to dress up in for a school play, a party, or a parade.

Use light-tan wrapping paper, or a piece of an old garment bag, about 24 inches square. Spread the paper out flat and draw Indian designs on it with colored crayon. Fold the square as in Figure 1, then fold again as in Figure 2. The heavy line shows how to cut the folded paper so it will fit around the neck. Slash the edges and cut a straight line up the front as in Figure 3.

Designs on a Bowl

By Ella L. Langenberg

Select a bowl which is wider at the top than the bottom. Rub vaseline or lard over the entire outside surface of the bowl. Cover this with cheesecloth, putting it on as smoothly as possible.

Spread some paste over the cloth. Tear or cut strips or wedge-shaped pieces of black-and-white newspaper. Place them over the paste, adding more paste when necessary. Use small pieces of paper to fill in.

Do not paste the paper over the open top edge of the bowl.

When the entire bowl has been covered with black-and-white pieces, spread paste over it, then cover it with a similar layer cut from colored newspaper. Continue in this way until there are eight or ten layers of paper. Put the bowl aside to dry.

When the paper is thoroughly dry, carefully loosen the top edge with a sharp knife. It should come off the bowl easily.

Paste paper pieces over the top rim of the paper bowl to make a firm edge. Smooth the outside with sandpaper. Lining paper may be pasted inside.

Paint the entire bowl, inside and outside, with tempera paint.

Several Indian designs and symbols are shown here. These symbols of nature, like the sun, mountains, animals, are represented in different ways by different tribes. They are not always the same in rugs, baskets, and pottery. Sometimes the designs are in outline, or in black and white, or in color.

Choose symbols and draw them on the paper bowl. Paint them with tempera paint.

When the paint is dry, give the entire bowl one or two coats of shellac. Be sure the first coat is thoroughly dry before putting on a second coat. The bowl should now be firm and glossy.

Katcina Doll

This doll is a milk or orange juice carton built up with papier mâché. Use two thin strips of wood or heavy cardboard for the feet. For the other features, roll or crumple paper to the right shape. Dip torn strips of paper toweling into wallpaper paste, and fasten the features in place. Then cover the entire doll with these strips until it is the right shape.

When the paste is thoroughly dry, decorate the doll with tempera paints. Finish with a coat of shellac. Add real feathers, or cut some from colored construction paper.

By Barbara Baker

Pilgrim Girl and Doll

The head is a wad of paper covered with a 3-inch circle of white crepe paper, fastened at the neck with wire. The arms are a roll of colored crepe paper, fastened at the wrist ends with wire, and attached to the neck.

The dress is a piece of crepe paper the same color as the arms. Cut a hole in the center and a slit up the back. Pull it down over the head and put a wire around the waistline. Add a white paper apron, and colored paper braids and bangs. Cover the head with a hood to match the dress. Paste on paper eyes and mouth.

Make the doll the same way. Fasten it to the girl's arms with wire.

Indian Peace Pipe

Use one or two straight, round sticks for the pipestem, and a paper cup or thread spool for the bowl. Add small pieces of wood for the raised places on the stem.

Dip torn strips of paper toweling into wallpaper paste, and wrap them around the pipe until it is built up to the desired size and shape.

Let it dry thoroughly, then decorate with tempera paints and touches of silver and gold. When the paint is dry, cover the pipe with a coat of shellac.

Tie on thongs made from shoelaces or strips of old leather. Trim the thongs with beads and feathers.

To Make for Christmas

Stained Glass Windows

By Judith LaDez

Draw the outline of the pictures on ordinary white paper, and go over them with black India ink on both sides of the paper. Spread cooking or mineral oil over the paper with cotton or fingers. Allow it to soak into the paper, then wipe off all excess oil until the paper is dry. Color the figures with crayons on both sides of the paper.

Wreath for Door or Window

By Barbara Mount

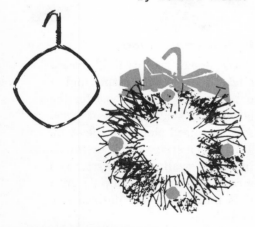

These wreaths are weatherproof for indoor or outdoor use. If they become crushed, all you need do is fluff them out with your hand and they are like new again.

Materials needed are one wire clothes hanger, plastic sheets or ten small plastic bags, one yard of 3-inch plastic ribbon, four medium-sized Christmas tree balls, and paint or fingernail polish to paint the handle of the hanger.

Form the hanger by grasping the hook in both hands and placing one foot on the lower wire. Stretch the hanger until it makes a square. Then, with the hands, round it into a circle. Paint the handle and let it dry.

Cut the plastic into strips 3 inches wide and 6 to 7 inches long. Tie these pieces onto the hanger, flaring the ends of the plastic as you tie. Push the knots together on the wire until it is completely covered.

Tie the ribbon in a bow around the hook. Run a short string through the loop on the Christmas balls, and tie one at the top and bottom, and one on either side of the wreath.

Many other ideas for decorating these wreaths will come after doing a few.

Candle Place Card

By M. Mable Lunz

Cut a 2-by-4-inch card from heavy construction paper. Remove the wire from a small Christmas tree ball and insert a birthday candle in the hole. Put a drop of household cement on the card and set the ball in the cement. Decorate the card around the ball. Write the guest's name on the card.

Angel
By Barbara Baker

Make the body and wings from a rectangle of white construction paper. Cut on a slant from the bottom corners to about a half inch from the top. Bend back the side pieces for wings. Scallop the bottom of the skirt. Trim with pink paper designs. Paste tiny yellow feet at the back of the skirt bottom.

For arms, slip a strip of white paper around the body. Bend the ends forward and paste them to a yellow paper book.

Cut a large yellow oval head with a tab for the neck. Snip around the oval and curl the ends forward for hair. Paste a pink circle face in the center, adding black paper fringed eyelashes and red mouth. Paste the tab neck to the body top, at the back.

Sewing Basket
By Dorothe A. Palms

Wash and dry a round half-gallon ice-cream carton. Cut a paper pattern that will cover the carton halfway around and from bottom to rolled-rim top. Cut two of these shapes from felt. Apply glue to the carton and place the felt pieces, one at a time, working from the bottom up and smoothing it out carefully. Tuck the top of the felt under the rolled rim of the carton.

Place the carton lid on felt, draw around it, and cut out the circle. Paste cotton to the lid top, mounting it higher at the center to form a pincushion effect. Cover the felt circle with glue and place it over the cotton, smoothing it out and poking the edges under the rolled rim of the lid.

Trim box and lid with rickrack and gummed stars. Cut three felt leaves and paste them, at the stem ends only, to the lid as shown. Make the rosebuds from short strips of rickrack, gluing one side, then rolling the strips tight. Paste them at the center of the leaf cluster.

The sample was made from green felt, with pink-and-silver rickrack and silver stars; but any color combination may be used.

Santa Scroll
By Ruth Everding Libbey

Use a piece of white cloth about 20 by 36 inches, perhaps from an old sheet. Stitch a hem at top and bottom wide enough to hold sticks. Draw the Santa and trees on the cloth with pencil, then color them with crayons—red suit and cap, black belt and boots, green trees. Glue on cotton whiskers, hair, and jacket trim, and a gold paper belt buckle. Sew a bell at the tip of the cap, or paste on a white cotton tassel. Slide the sticks through the top and bottom hems. Tie on a red string or yarn hanger as shown. Hang the scroll on the wall or the front door.

Egg Carton Bells
By James W. Perrin, Jr.

Use the papier-mâché type of egg carton. Cut out the cup shapes and trim the rough edges. Punch a small hole in the top of each bell. Paint the bells with poster paints, or cover them with foil, or dip them in glitter. Decorate them with all sorts of objects from the scrap box. Small Christmas balls can be added as clappers.

Force a piece of yarn, with a knot on one end, through the punched hole in each bell. Tie several bells together in a group. Hang them on the tree, or use them for any Christmas decorating.

Gifts To Make

A Cooky Drum
By Gladys L. Martin

Tasty homemade cookies make Christmas gifts anyone will like. Wrap them to look like a drum. Cookies about 3 inches across will make the best-looking drum. If they are crumbly, wrap each one separately in waxed paper before stacking them.

Cut two circles of cardboard large enough to extend over the edges of the cookies. Cover the circles with bright-colored paper or Christmas paper. If preferred, these circles may be cut from colored paper plates. Make slots near the edges of the circles.

Place one circle on top of the stack of cookies, the other on the bottom. Lace the two circles together with ribbon drawn through the slots from one circle to the other as shown.

Decorate the top circle with Christmas seals or colored cutouts. If the drum is to be hung on the Christmas tree, run a string through the center of the top circle before lacing the circles together.

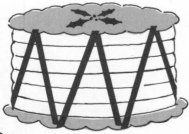

A Doll's Tea Set
By Barbara Gilpin

This tea set is made from the cup sections of an egg carton. Trim off the top edges so they are smooth and even. Cut the handles from the carton lid.

Make four teacups with handles, as shown.

For the creamer, pinch the top of the cup together on one side to form the pouring lip. Paste the handle on the side opposite the pouring lip.

For the sugar bowl, paste two handles on opposite sides of the cup.

For the Lazy Susan, cut off a 4-cup section from the carton. Make the handle from a 12-inch piece of light wire. Fold it double and twist it to form a handle as shown. Punch the ends of the wire through the center section between the four cups. Bend the wire on the underside so it cannot pull out. A piece of gummed tape will hold it in place. Use it to serve nuts, candy, or popcorn.

Paint the set with water colors or tempera paint.

Bunny Pencil Holder
By Agnes Choate Wonson

On a 5-inch piece of cardboard tubing, sketch eyes, nose, and feet. Color the tubing light brown with crayon. Add brown paper ears and broomstraw whiskers.

Glue the tube to a slightly larger circle for a base. At the back, add a wad of cotton for the bunny's tail.

Some Gift Ideas
By Ruth Boone

These three gifts are made from the bottoms of empty food cans.

To cut off a bottom neatly, with no sharp edges, put the can into the opener on its side and cut around the bottom just below the rim.

Water-glass Cover. Use the bottom of a can that measures about 3 inches across. Paint it with colored enamel. Paint a small thread spool in a contrasting color.

When dry, glue the spool to the center of the cover on the plain side. The rim on the underside will keep the cover from sliding off the glass.

Find a fancy button a little

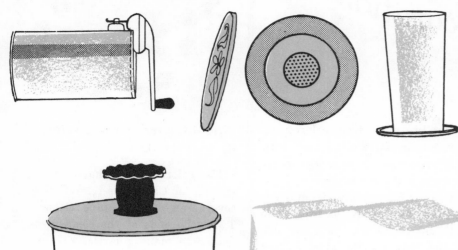

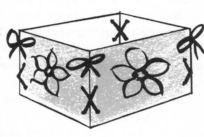

larger than the top of the spool
—the kind with the hole underneath instead of through the
button. Glue it on top of the
spool over the hole.

Teapot Stand. Use the bottom
of an empty coffee can that
measures about 5 inches across.
Paint as before, and let dry.

Cover the rim side with a circle
of felt or flannel. Paste a pretty
cutout on the other side.

On the back, near the edge,
glue a cloth picture hanger from
the dime store, so the stand may
be hung on the wall when not
in use.

Coaster Set. Make a set of six
coasters to use under glasses on
the table.

Use the bottoms from 3-inch
cans. If desired, paint each one
a different color.

Turn them rim side up and
paint a bird or a flower in the
center. Or paint rings of different colors, following the raised
rings in the metal. The raised
rings keep the coaster from sticking to the glass.

Trinket Box
By Evelyn Cook

Materials: a half-pint milk
carton; wallpaper, poster paper,
or colored paper from a magazine; four 8-inch pieces of yarn.

Cut away the top of the milk
carton so that a 2-inch-high box
is left. Cut down from top to
bottom on each corner.

Cut four pieces of colored paper, 3 by 4 inches, to cover the
sides of the box. Cut another
piece to fit the bottom of the box.

Glue the four pieces over the
sides of the box.

Punch three holes along the
corner edges of the box as shown.
Lace the corners together with
yarn, beginning at the bottom
and working up as for lacing
shoes. Tie a perky little bow at
the top.

When the lacing is finished on
all four corners, glue the piece of
colored paper on the bottom of
the box.

Hot-dish Mat
By Irene K. Koffarnus

Seven milk-bottle caps will
make a hot-dish mat for use on
the table.

Remove the cardboard circle
inside each cap. Paint the bottom
side of each circle with tempera
or enamel, using a color that
looks well with the color of the
cap.

Place **one cap** on a piece of
cardboard, **and** arrange six more
around it. Each cap should touch
the center one and those on each
side of it. Trace around this arrangement on the cardboard, and
cut it out. Paint it either the
same color as the milk-bottle caps
or as the circles.

After the paint is dry, sew the
caps to the cardboard with heavy
thread. Cross two stitches in
each cap to make the mat sturdy.

Glue felt or flannel to the
bottom of the cardboard. Then
replace the painted circles in the
caps.

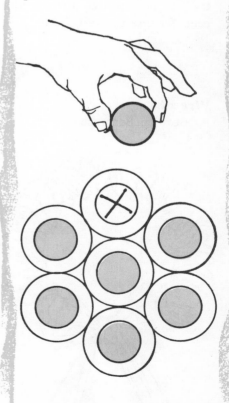

Christmas Decorations

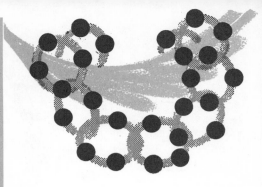

Candy Cane Mobile
By Barbara Baker

Cut a 6-inch cane from red construction paper. Wrap it with ¼-inch-wide white paper as shown, creasing it flat as you wrap. Paste the two ends of the strip to the cane, leaving the rest free.

Wreaths
By Beatrice Bachrach

Cut two stars from colored paper. Slit in halfway on each star, and slip one slit into the other to make a double star.

Cut the Santa shape from a triangle of red paper. Decorate it on both sides. Cut up along one side of the body for the arm, cutting off the strip at the proper length, and adding a white mitten. Toward the top of the Santa, cut out a nose shape. Slip white paper under it, and cut to the shape shown.

Cut two green Christmas trees. Staple together up the middle. Bend the four halves to stand out.

Tie a string through the top of each of these units, attaching the other end of the string to a white strip on the cane. Vary the lengths of the strings as shown. Tie a string hanger to the ends of the cane.

Cut a wreath shape from construction paper. Cut squares of colored facial tissue, about 2 by 2 inches.

Put a dab of paste in the center of a tissue square. Paste it on the wreath. Ruffle the edges. Apply paste to another square and place it as close to the first square as possible. Continue this until the wreath is completed.

Add berries of another color, and a large bow.

If a more elaborate wreath is desired, make two wreaths as described, and staple or paste them together, back to back.

Pipe Cleaner Bead Chain
By M. Mable Lunz

Use colored beads that come in strings for Christmas trim. String several on a white pipe cleaner. Twist the ends of the cleaner together to make a circle. Fill another pipe cleaner, stick it through the first circle, and twist the ends together. Continue making the chain to the desired length.

These are very effective on the Christmas tree, or strung around the room.

Door Decoration
By Margarett E. Gretchen

Cut out a large boot from red oilcloth. Write an appropriate greeting on it. Cut a smaller boot for each member of the family with a name on each boot. Outline all the boots with snow spray.

Attach the large boot to the center of the door. Arrange the rest of the boots around it.

30

Paper Santas for Christmas Trim

By Barbara Baker

Triangles make this Santa, two red, and one white slashed around edges. Cutout features. Eyebrows slashed to stick up. Add boots, belt, and pompon.

A Santa from paper stapled together in a tube. Arms, a hollow square of paper fastened to back. Cone hat, white trim. Add eyes, eyebrows, beard, belt, and boots.

Red Santa face, cotton-trimmed. Cutout nose folded to stand out. Fasten at top to white background which carries Christmas message.

A fat Santa. Round white face with slashed edge. Eyebrows cut around edge to stick up. Any expression desired. Round body with black boots and belt. Add buckle and pompon.

A tall accordion-pleated triangle Santa. He carries black bag and wears black boots. White tube face, pasted at back. White pompon.

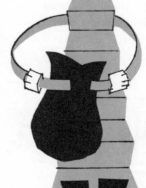

31

For the Door or Fireplace

By Betsy Jane Boyd

Punch a hole in the bottom of three small tin cans. Paint and decorate them in gay colors. Use tiny Christmas balls for clappers, suspending them in the can by narrow ribbon. Tie the ribbon ends to a spray of pine. Add a large ribbon bow and a cluster of balls, as shown.

Table Favors

By Betsy Jane Boyd

Cover a cardboard tube and a round cardboard base with metallic paper. Run a string through a Christmas tree ball, down through the tube and base. Use gummed tape or nail polish for the features. Paste on metallic paper wings. Trim with tinsel as shown. Make one for each guest.

A Menorah for Hanukkah

By Betsy Jane Boyd

On a sheet of heavy construction paper paste strips of dark gummed tape in the shape of a Menorah. Make the center holder for the Shamas candle a little higher than the rest. Cut the candles from orange gummed tape, making them narrower than the candleholders. Add the flames with colored crayon.

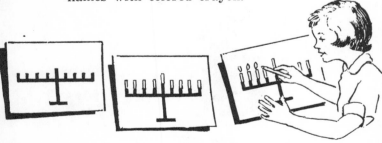

Room Decorations

By Betsy Jane Boyd

Decorate several Christmas tree balls. Make the features from bits of colored gum tape, or paint on with nail polish. Paste on yarn hair or curls from a metallic pot scraper. Trim with ribbon or cloth scraps. Hang them on a long cord.

A Wreath for Your Room

By Georgena Goff

The wreath is made from a round foil coffee cake container.

On a sheet of paper, trace a circle the size of the bottom of the container. Within the circle, draw a five-pointed star pattern. Trace the star onto the bottom of the foil container.

Cut out the sections AROUND the star. Be careful to leave each star point attached to the dish.

Decorate the star with tinsel, holding it in place with paper clips. Attach a ribbon at the top for hanging. A hole may be made in the bottom of the wreath for an electric bulb, if desired.

Christmas Tree Decoration

By Merle Wolf

From colored construction paper or from silver, gold or colored heavy foil, cut seven circles, 2 inches in diameter. Fold six of the circles in half. Cut a slit in each from the center of the fold toward the curve of the circle, as shown. With the circles still folded, slip the slits onto the remaining flat circle. Space the six circles evenly, then spread them open a bit. Attach a string hanger.

32

Christmas Trees From Paper

These trees make festive holiday table decorations. They can be made from colored construction, metallic, or other interesting paper. Three of the trees shown are built upon a cone shape. The other one is formed by cutting and bending.

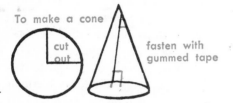

To make a cone

cut out

fasten with gummed tape

For tree No. 1, make rings of graduated widths from different-colored paper, fitting them to the cone shape from bottom to top. For the branches, fold strips of paper as shown, gluing the ends together. Vary the length of the branches for interest. Glue the tab to the ring. Decorate with paper circles, gummed stars, or sequins.

Tree No. 2 is also decorated with rings of graduated widths. Glued to the inside of each ring is a wider ring of contrasting color which has been cut to points. The points are bent forward. Small circles are glued to the cone between the rings. The bottom of the cone is cut as shown.

Tree No. 3 requires no pasting. Cut circles of graduated sizes from the pattern shown. Slash and bend as pictured. Decorate if desired.

Tree No. 4 is made from a triangle. Fold in half and cut slits as shown. Open triangle and bend forward every other strip. Decorate as desired.

Adapted from "Creating With Paper" by Pauline Johnson, published by the University of Washington Press, Seattle, Washington.

glue

tab

1

2

cut out

Cut on solid lines. Fold on dotted lines.

3

fold

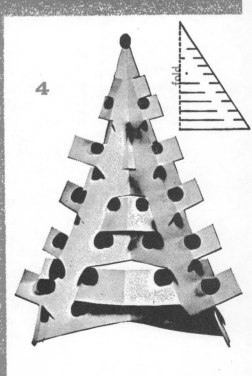

4

Christmas

Clip-ons
By Barbara Baker

These party and tray favors are made over clip-on clothespins and can be worn later. Since half the fun is in the making, why not assemble the material and let the guests make their own clip-ons as one of the party games?

Cut Santas, angels, wreaths, stockings, or trees from colored felt or metallic paper. Use cotton or yarn for whiskers and hair; sequins or stars for eyes and mouths; pipe cleaners for arms; tinsel, shiny paper, bits of lace-paper doily, and glitter, for trim. Use rubber cement to paste the parts in place. Stick each favor into a small hunk of clay and set it on a paper doily or small dish.

Christmas Bells
By Ella L. Langenberg

Select a bell-shaped form such as a small glass, plastic dish, or flowerpot. Be sure the sides slope gently from top to bottom. Turn it upside down like a bell. Rub vaseline generously over the entire outside of the object.

Tear newspaper into small pieces. They need not have a definite form. Put the paper in two piles, one of black-and-white pieces, the other colored.

Use wallpaper paste, or make a thin solution of flour-and-water mixture.

Spread a layer of paper napkin over the vaseline. Be sure there are no wrinkles in this layer.

Now paste the newspaper on, first a layer of black-and-white, then a layer of color. Do not paste any paper over the edge. Three or four layers will make a thin bell, six or seven will make a heavier bell.

Set the bell aside to dry. It may take more than a day. Drying may be hastened by placing the object near heat.

Loosen the bottom edge of the paper with a knife point. The paper shell should slip off easily. Sandpaper any rough places. Paint with tempera or gold. Use plain, or trim with stars, sequins, or glitter. Make a loop with wire, a hairpin, or thread.

Reindeer Cutouts
By Agnes Choate Wonson

Cut a strip of heavy wrapping paper 16 inches long, 3½ inches wide. Fold it in half three times. With the folds at the sides, draw a reindeer's head. Bring the tip of the nose and two antlers to the edge of the right side, and two antlers to the edge of the left side, as shown by the dotted lines.

Cut out along the solid lines only. The dotted lines form the hinges that hold the chain together.

Open the chain. Paint the antlers, nostrils, and eyes. Put white paint in the eye centers.

Gift Tags or Place Cards
By Ella L. Langenberg

These cards are made from red, green, or white construction paper, 2½ by 7 inches, folded with the short edges together. Cut two slits on the folded edge as shown. Roll the middle section forward with a pencil to form a loop.

Write the name neatly on the card, using ink or tempera paint of contrasting color. Put a twig of evergreen or other trim through the loop.

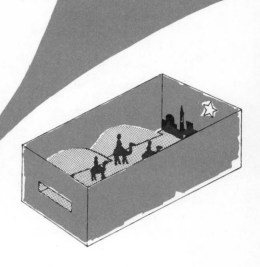

Tree Mobiles
By Barbara Baker

Cut a green construction paper triangle, higher than it is wide across the bottom. A 5½-inch triangle, for instance, should be 4 inches across the bottom. Any size can be used, even up to 18 inches high.

Cut the triangle into strips, crosswise as shown, leaving a triangle top. Arrange the strips in order, with space between as illustrated. Lay a long piece of colored string up the middle and paste it to the pieces with gummed tape. Leave enough string at the top to make a hanger, and enough at the bottom to attach the base.

Cut the base on a fold of construction paper. Run the bottom of the string through a hole in the center of the base fold. Knot the string inside the fold, then paste the base together at the bottom.

Decorate the strips on both sides with sequins, stars, glitter, or anything that shines.

When these tree mobiles are hung, the strips will swing in different directions.

Christmas Peep Show
By Sylvia Pezoldt

Use a box about the size of a shoe box. In the middle of one end cut a slot about 3 inches long and an inch wide, spaced for good viewing. Discard the lid. Cover the box with colored paper or Christmas wrapping paper.

Before covering the top, arrange the scene. Remember that the viewer will be looking through the slot as down an aisle, so the edges of the scenery must be glued to the sides of the box to stand out.

For the ground of the scene, use sand-colored paper to represent smooth, wind-swept desert country. Cut some rounded hills of the same paper to paste on both sides of the box.

A silhouette of a city with flat roofs and a few rounded towers to represent an ancient Biblical city can be cut from black construction paper, and pasted low against the back of the box. Place a brilliant star above the city, using glitter or silver paper. The correct position is supposed to be at the right where the wise men saw it. The three kings on their camels could be cut from a Christmas card, or plain black silhouettes may be cut from construction paper. Space them among the sand hills, journeying toward the star.

Finish with a cover of yellow tissue paper over the top of the box. Now peep through the slot and see how interesting this scene is. Last, cover the top with plain tissue paper, put on very smoothly so that the light can come through to make it look like the sky.

35

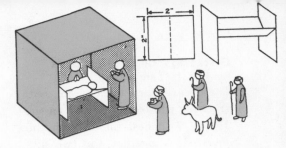

Angel Plaques
By Texie Hering

Cut a pink construction paper foundation in the shape of a church window, and a white frame as shown. Glue the three corners of the frame to the foundation. Cut the white angel and glue the body center to the foundation center. Bend out the wings and the head a little. Leave as a silhouette or crayon yellow hair, and use black ink for eyes, nose, and mouth. Cut the tab as shown. Glue or tape it to the back.

Paper Plate Wreath
By Luella Pierce

Cut out the center of a 9-inch paper plate. Cut a strip of dark-green crepe paper 2 inches wide and 10 feet long, or just long enough to wrap around the plate rim. Make slashes along one side of the strip about ¾ inch deep and ¼ inch apart. Wrap it around the rim as shown, and fasten with glue or scotch tape. Add a bow of red crepe paper.

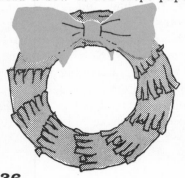

Cooky Cutter Candles
By Margaret Squires

Materials needed are cooky cutters of tree, bell, and star shapes; a cake or jelly roll pan; green, red, and white candles (white candles may be colored with scrapings from wax crayons); sequins and narrow red and white ribbon for trim.

Melt the candles, one color at a time, slowly so the wax will not get too hot. Lift out the wicks and lay them aside to be used later. Pour the wax into a cake or jelly roll pan—enough so it will be a little over ¼ inch thick. Set it aside until it is firm but not completely cool.

Always cut out an even number of shapes. It will take two shapes with a wick between to make one candle. Press the cooky cutter into the wax. Lift out the shape with a wide spatula.

On half of the shapes, lay a piece of the wick from the bottom to the top, as in Figure 1. Melt the excess wax left in the pan. Put ½ teaspoonful of it onto each shape with a wick. Place the rest of the shapes over these, one by one. Press down gently until the two halves are one.

Pour the rest of the melted wax into the pan. Let it stand until firm. Cut out oblong pieces, a little larger than the bottom of the shapes, and mold a base onto the bottom of each candle, as shown.

Trim both sides of each candle. Some suggestions are pictured. Run small pins through sequins to hold ribbon and other trim in place.

Miniature Creche
By Sylvia Pezoldt

This inexpensive creche may be moved around, and added to as the Christmas season advances.

A cardboard box about 4 inches square will make the stable. Cover it with brown paper or color it with brown crayon or water colors. Stand it on edge, leaving the front open.

Shred yellow paper for straw to scatter inside and in front of the stable. Make the manger from a 2-inch square of brown cardboard folded to make a trough. Paste squares of cardboard on each end to make it stand.

To make the figures, bend pipe cleaners to form the bodies. Dress them with bits of crepe paper or cloth. A ball of modeling clay or small gumdrops for feet will help the figure stand. Heads may be a wooden bead, clay, or faces cut out from Christmas cards or magazines. Glue them to the top of the pipe cleaner. Add a headdress to make shepherds and kings. To find ideas for headdresses and costumes, look at Christmas cards. Animals are made with pipe cleaners, or pictures can be cut from cards and attached to standards.

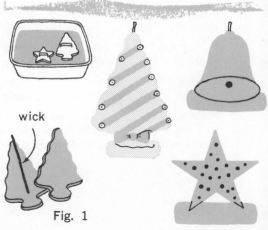

wick

Fig. 1

Christmas Cards

By Agnes Choate Wonson

Cancelled stamps are used to create these clever little Christmas cards. Cut holly leaves from green stamps, berries from red stamps, and a bow from a blue stamp. Lightly pencil a circle on the card and paste the parts over it to form the wreath. Use red crayon to write the message and dot the edge of the card.

Cut three candles from green, the flames from tan, and the bases from blue, and paste on the second card as shown. Use blue crayon for the message and for dotting the card edge.

Colors and designs may be varied as desired.

By Ella L. Langenberg

For the tree, cut three squares of green paper in three sizes. Fold each square in half and cut along the heavy line as shown. Cut strips of green paper for the tree trunk, and a base for the tree to stand on.

Cut a piece of white or light-colored paper for the card. Paste the tree to the card, starting with the base and trunk, and adding the overlapping triangles as illustrated.

Trim the tree with candles and little triangle shades, using silver, gold, red, or white paper. Paste the candles in rows or groups to make the card look pretty.

By Ella L. Langenberg

Cut a piece of white construction paper about 6 by 9 inches. Fold it to make a folder 6 by 4½ inches.

On the top page of the folder draw a house with the side on the folded edge as shown by the dotted line. Draw a door, a large window, two small windows, and a chimney. Leave the house plain white, or color it. Draw lines to look like clapboard, shingle, or brick. Cut out the house shape through both pages, leaving the folded side uncut.

Working on the top page only, cut the door on three sides. Fold along the fourth side so it will open and close. Decorate it as desired.

Cut the windows completely out. Paste clear cellophane back of them for glass. Cut and paste candles on the back of the two small windows. Write a Christmas message along the bottom of the card.

On the inside page of the folder paste a Christmas tree cut from green construction paper. Make it large enough to show through the windows and door as shown. Trim the tree with bits of colored and shiny paper.

Cut-and-paste Cards
By Barbara Baker

Make white folders. Decorate them with tiny pieces of colored crepe, metallic, or colored paper, sequins, and lines of ink.

The wise men, shepherds, Mary and Joseph, are long triangles. Their heads are tiny circles made with a hole puncher. The babe is a tiny triangle with little gold halo. A long triangular piece of crepe paper, shaped as shown, makes the roof of the stable, with a short piece on each side. Put a couple of shiny stars in the sky.

Cut out a city and fly a Santa and reindeer over it. Draw the reindeer as simply as possible. Draw Santa in a sleigh. Put cotton over the sleigh so only Santa's nose and cap are showing.

For Rudolph, cut seven small strips of brown crepe paper. Glue them to the card. He's fun and easy to make. Tiny pieces make little horns like the branches of a tree. Don't forget his red nose of bright-red paper, and have one eye peer out at you.

From brown crepe paper cut a triangle for the roof of the creche. Shape as shown. Cut straight pieces for the sides. Make the manger of dark paper, the straw of yellow. Cut the animals, some lying down and some standing up. Put a moon and a large star in the sky. Paste them in position.

38

Waxed Paper Greeting Cards   By Lillie D. Chaffin

Cut double waxed-paper cards in fancy shapes—stars, circles, triangles, or Santas. If they are to be mailed, cut the cards to fit the envelopes.

For each card, draw a picture and cut it out, or use cutouts from magazines. Decorate with bits of cloth, cotton, gummed stars, and the like. Add a greeting, and sign

your name in colored crayon.

Lay the design between the pieces of waxed paper and press with a warm iron. Finish the edges with pinking shears if desired.

Santa Cards   By Barbara Baker

The illustrations show how easy it is to make simple, attractive greeting cards.   Make the folder card first, then cut decorations to

fit. The large parts may be cut from colored felt, gummed paper, or cloth. The features may be sequins or metallic paper, with white

cotton whiskers and fur.

Try some original designs, using material on hand, and see what fun it is to use your own ideas.

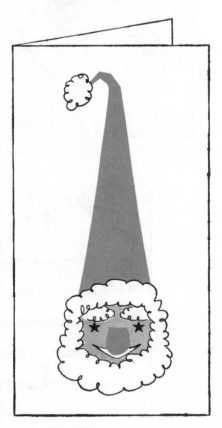

Christmas Packages

Gift Bags
By Bernice Walz

Choose the right-sized brown or white paper bag to hold the gift. Decorate the sides of the bag with strips of leftover ribbon or foil from gift packages. Use cutouts of letters from old Christmas cards to make greetings. Colorful designs or figures from cards can be used effectively. These can be glued over the ribbon trim if desired.

Mount cutouts on a harmonizing piece of bright Christmas foil wrap, then cut out, leaving about ¼ inch of the foil for a border.

Trim the top of the bag with ribbon strips. Scallop the top edges, or trim straight across. Use bows from old packages, tinsel, or any odds and ends, to add your own decorative touch.

Angel Package Decoration
By Bernice Walz

Make the face from a circle of Christmas sheet cotton, a milk filter, or soft cotton paper from a candy box. Draw eyes with colored pencil or crayon. For the mouth, paste on a bit of red construction paper. Add curls from a metallic scouring pad. Cut two wings from the material used for the face.

Wrap the Christmas package in plain colored paper. Secure the ends with cellophane tape. Paste the head and wings in place on the top of the package. Add a gold paper halo and a little ribbon bow at the neck.

This angel also may be used on colored construction paper to make an attractive Christmas card.

Gift Containers
By Virginia Follis

These lovely gift boxes may be made from plain white frozen-food boxes.

Wash and dry the box. If it is not glued together, spread it apart and paint it with thick tempera or poster paints. Dip the wet brush occasionally in a small amount of scouring powder to make the paint stay on the waxed surface. If there is any printing on the box, several coats of paint may be needed.

Make all the brush strokes in the same direction. Brush strokes may resemble the grain in wood. When the paint is dry, shellac the box.

Before putting the box back together, glue Christmas decorations on the lid with airplane or household cement.

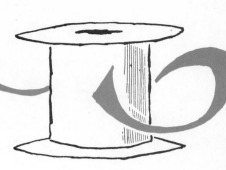

Wrappings

By Betsy Ann Page

By Betsy Ann Page

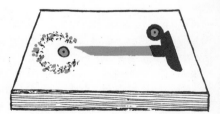

Materials: green, red, white tissue paper; green, red, white felt; pipe cleaners, paper doilies, sequins, glitter, clear china cement.

Wrap gift boxes in tissue paper. Use these decorating suggestions, or try original designs. Don't wipe off excess cement. Let it dry and it won't show.

Cut out two red felt bells and two green felt bells. Cut off bottoms of green bells. Glue green bells on red bells. Add sequin clappers. Cut pipe cleaner to desired length. Bend ends to form circles. Glue to box. Decorate cleaner with glitter. Glue bells under circles.

Bend pipe cleaners to form letters. Glue to box. Add star sections cut from paper doily. Decorate with sequins.

Remove center from paper doily. Glue remaining circle to box. Add cutout star to center. Decorate with colored sequins.

White felt snow men. Colored felt hats, cane, and muff. Ribbon scarves. Crayon features and sequin buttons. Run length of pipe cleaner through snow men to form arms. Add feather or glitter decoration to hat. Glue snow men to box.

Green felt candleholder. Red felt candle. Glue to box. Add circle of glitter around sequin flame.

February Make-It Fun

Three Hearts

By Margaret Squires

This valentine novelty can be used as a favor or as a valentine to be mailed.

Cut a piece of red construction paper 8 by 6 inches. Fold in half to 4 by 6 inches. Measure up ¾ inch from the fold on each side and draw a line across the paper. Fold each side back along the line. There are now three folds. The first or middle fold is between the other two. Spread the paper slightly to be sure it will stand alone on the two folds, as shown.

Cut three different-sized heart patterns. Arrange them on the folded paper so the points are a half inch from the bottom. Trace around the hearts. With folds together, start at the edge and cut out around the hearts as shown by the heavy line. Do not cut the points shown by the dotted line.

With white paint or ink, outline the point of each heart, adding your own decorations. Write a valentine message on the hearts.

Glue the backs of the hearts together at the top. Spread at the bottom so it will stand on the two folded edges.

Newspaper Jungle

By Lois Marie Fink

Animals of all kinds can be made from newspaper, string, toothpicks, and tempera paint.

First decide on the kind of animal to make. Think about the shape. How thick is its body? How long is its neck?

For an animal shaped like a horse, make two long, thin rolls of newspaper. These will be the legs. Put a fatter roll around the middle of the two long rolls to hold them in place and to form the body. Tie this fat roll at each end with string, not too tightly. Make another roll for the neck. Push it into the body in the right position. Fold over the end of the neck and flatten it out for the head. Stick in two toothpicks for ears. Make the tail from string, or fringe a piece of paper.

Now color the animal. With stripes he could be a zebra. With spots he could be a dappled horse. Or make a fantastic animal with bright polka dots and toothpick whiskers.

Make several animals, then make a jungle home for them. Trees and grass can be made from newspaper,

too. A roll of newspaper can be the tree trunk. Tear the end into long strips to form the limbs and leaves. To make the trees stand, tie string around the bottom of the trees and around a big piece of cardboard. Fasten them to the cardboard with long strips of transparent gummed tape. Use the cardboard as the ground of the jungle.

Now start out without any idea of a certain kind of animal. Just form a body and legs with the newspaper, and see what kind of fantastic animal can be made!

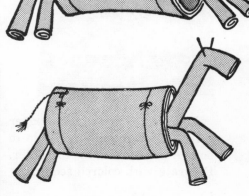

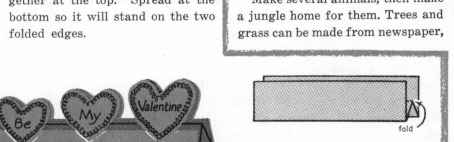

fold

42

A Patriotic Valentine

By Carol Conner

Cut a piece of white construction paper 5 by 7 inches. Fold it in half to 3½ by 5 inches.

With the paper folded, draw a light pencil line along the 5-inch side, a half inch in from the edge. Then, from the fold to the border line, draw nine parallel lines, a half inch apart, starting a half inch from the edge. With the paper still folded, begin at the fold and cut along each parallel line, as shown.

Cut ten strips of blue paper, each ½ inch wide and 5 inches long. Open the folder, and weave the first blue strip over and under the slits. Push it tightly against the edge. Weave the second blue strip, making it go over where the first went under, and under where the first went over. Weave in five strips to the fold. Then start from the opposite end and weave the other side of the folder in the same way.

On the inside of the folder bend the loose ends back from the mar-

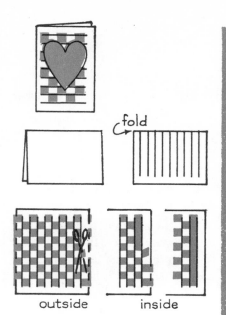

fold

outside   inside

gin. This brings all the blue ends on the inside of the folder in an even row. Paste them in place. Cut off the opposite ends even with the border.

Cut a piece of white paper 5 by 7 inches. Paste it over the inside of the folder. Write a valentine message or verse on it.

Fold a piece of red construction paper and cut a half heart. Open it and paste on the front of the folder.

Press the open folder under a heavy book until dry.

Valentine Doll

By Ruth Dougherty

For the body, cut out a large red construction paper heart, about 6 inches across.

Cut two smaller white hearts for the head. On one heart paste fringed eyelashes cut from black paper, and a red paper mouth.

Cut lengths of yellow paper ribbon and curl by drawing them over a scissor blade, to represent hair. Paste the ends as shown to the back of the heart face. Then paste the second white heart over the back of the head to keep the curls in place.

Cut legs and arms the right sizes

and shapes. Fasten these and the head in place with two-prong paper fasteners.

Paste a tiny white heart on the doll's body, and write a valentine message on it. Run a string through the top of the head to hang up the doll.

Wax Flowers

By Katherine Bartow

Arrange a tree branch in a small flowerpot or vase filled with pebbles to hold it firm.

Melt old candles in small juice cans, placed in a pan of hot water over a low flame. Paraffin melted with bits of colored crayon may be used, instead.

Shape the end of a raw carrot to the desired shape and size. It may be cone-shaped or cup-shaped. Use a small, thin carrot for small flowers; a fat one for large flowers.

Dip the shaped end of the carrot in a glass of cold water, then into melted wax. Dip again in cold water so the wax will set faster. The deeper the carrot is dipped in the wax, the larger the flower will be.

When the wax has set, twist it slightly to loosen, and remove it from the carrot. If the wax is cone-shaped, press the point around the branch. If cup-shaped, press it firmly to the branch. Practice will help in finding the correct temperature. If the wax is too soft, the flower will collapse and lose its shape. If too cold, it won't stick.

Small flowers may be placed inside large ones for an interesting double effect. Flowers may be pressed into different shapes while warm—for instance, fluted sweet peas.

These wax flowers may be combined with fresh flowers or potted plants. Tiny flowers on a small sprig may be placed in a nut cup for table favors.

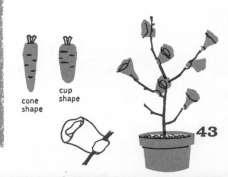

cone shape

cup shape

Valentine Bouquets

By Ruth Dougherty

Hearts cut from red, green, and white construction paper make the flowers for these valentine bouquets. Stems are white or green pipe cleaners pasted or stapled between two or more hearts. Pots are made from spools, or are small pots filled with colored pebbles.

For each flower of the bouquet, Figure 1, use two small red paper hearts with larger white crepe-paper hearts between. Cut a fancy edge around the white heart. Make each edge different.

For the bouquet, Figure 2, cut red, green, and white hearts. Make the green hearts larger. Decorate the white heart and write a message on it. Paste the white heart on the green, then the pipe-cleaner stem, then the red heart.

For each flower in Figure 3, cut two large red hearts. Paste one on each side of a paper doily with a green pipe-cleaner stem between. Write a message on a smaller white heart. Paste it to one of the red hearts.

To decorate spools or pots, fold a paper napkin in half four times, round off the point, and cut holes along the edges. Unfold, and tie it around the spool or pot. Or decorate with foil or bright-colored paper.

For the bush, Figure 4, tie small red hearts to twigs. Fill the pot with pebbles or lentils to hold the twigs in place.

Valentine Scatter Pins

By M. Mable Lunz

Cut the ends off popsicle sticks as shown. Place them together to form a heart. Paint with red nail polish. It will hold the pieces together. Let dry thoroughly, then give it a second coat.

Cut a 3-inch length of ¼-inch black or white ribbon. Fold it in half. Make a small bow of another piece and sew it to the top of the fold. Sew a small safety pin to the back of the bow. Glue the red heart to the bottom of the ribbon.

Make two or more to wear like scatter pins.

Party Heart Picks

By Margaret Squires

Use these picks to decorate a valentine cake or to stick through party sandwiches.

For the white-edged pick, cut one heart from red construction paper, and one from thin white paper. Fasten the end of a toothpick to the back of the red heart with gummed tape. Cut out the center of the white heart. Glue the remaining edge to the front of the red heart.

For the other pick, cut out three red hearts. To the back of one heart fasten a toothpick as before. Fold the other two hearts in half. Glue one half of each heart to each side of the first heart at the back. Then glue the remaining two halves together. This forms a three-sided heart which covers the top of the first heart.

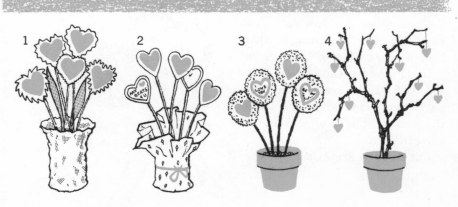

44

Milk Carton Plant Holder
By M. Mable Lunz

Measure 5 inches up from the bottom all around an empty milk carton. Cut off along this line. The bottom half of the carton is the plant holder. Cut a piece of colored construction paper about 8½ by 11 inches. Fold the 11-inch side around the holder, so the open edges meet at a corner. Crease it along the edges. Let the rest stick up over the top of the holder. With scotch tape, seal 2 inches of the construction paper at the bottom of the planter.

Cut down the corners of the paper and planter to 2 inches from the bottom. Fold the extra paper down over the inside of the four sides and fasten the ends in place.

Roll the four sides down around a pencil to make them curl, as shown.

Crepe-paper Fun
By Bernice Kimball

Cut pink, white, and green crepe paper into tiny pieces. Put them together in a box.

From brown construction paper cut a trunk of a tree about 4 inches long. Paste it on a sheet of 9-by-12-inch construction paper. Draw branches lightly in pencil. Put paste on the shape of the branches, and sprinkle the snippings on. It will look like an apple tree in blossom.

Paste different-colored snippings on a string to look like a vine.

Put glue on dry weeds, and sprinkle with yellow or red to make hollyhocks and the like.

Candy Cart
By Bernice Walz

Use a small nut cup for the cart. Pound a hole through the center of two metal bottle caps, to use for wheels. Cover the bottle caps with a piece of bright-colored foil, folding it over the edges to hold in place. Line the inside of the bottle cap with a different color foil paper.

Insert a pipe cleaner through the nut cup, about ½ inch from the bottom. Run the wheels on the pipe cleaner, one on either side of the cart. Bend the pipe cleaner ends over to hold the wheels securely.

Insert the pipe-cleaner tongue through the front part of the cart. Bend the end over the pipe cleaner inside the cart. Paste a small piece of pipe cleaner across the end of the tongue to form a handle.

Fill the cup with small candies. Use as a party or tray favor.

A Useful Gift
By Ella L. Langenberg

Select a top from a cardboard container that will fit over a water glass. Wash and dry it.

Draw and paint a design on the top with tempera paints. A flower, fruit, or a tree design are suggestions. The rim may be painted with lines, dots, or other shapes that look well with the design on the top.

When the paint is dry, give the entire lid a coat of shellac. Let it dry thoroughly.

The lid is to be used as a protection for a drinking glass. It may be placed on a bedside table or in a sickroom. It is sure to be a welcome gift.

Candy Valentines

Make a candy container from construction paper, using the pattern on the squared diagram. Cut on the black lines, fold on the dotted lines, and paste together. Color the hearts in a contrasting shade and decorate them as desired. Punch holes at the top of the hearts and tie together with a ribbon bow.

A larger container can be made from a paper bag. Cut off the top and decorate as shown.

Lollipops can be used, too. Cut two paper hearts and paste them together with the lollipop stick between. Or cut two hearts, one smaller than the other. Run the stick through the smaller heart and paste the larger one to it, as illustrated.

Wrap candy balls in colored cellophane and tie with colored string. Paste the string to a large paper heart, using a tiny heart for a sticker.

Hearty Clowns

By Opal Hoagland

Use shiny red ribbons saved from Christmas packages to make valentines. Use two 10-inch lengths of ribbon. Knot them together in two places. Paste small hearts at the ribbon ends for hands and feet. Paste on a heart face, and a half-heart for each ear. Add pointed cap and big collar.

Or make just the top part with ribbon arms and paste it on a large valentine.

For a table favor, cut two little notches in the collar, fit it over the back edge of a nut cup, and tape in place. Fill the cup with candy hearts.

Print the name of the guest on the collar and it will also serve as a place card.

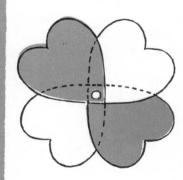

Four Leaf Clover Valentine

By Thelma T. Royer

Cut a pattern from newspaper, 3 by 3¾ inches.

Cut two hearts from red construction paper and two from white. Punch a small hole ½ inch from the point of each heart. Using first a red heart and then a white, overlap the hearts as shown. Push a two-pronged brass fastener through the holes, and spread the prongs.

On each heart, print a line of the following verse:

My heart for you, dear Mother,
With love is running over.
'Twould take four hearts to hold it,
So they're in this four-leaf clover.

Woven Heart Party Favor

By Thelma T. Royer

From white construction paper cut a heart 4 by 5 inches. Fold lengthwise, and measure, mark, and cut for weaving, as shown.

From red construction paper cut ½-inch strips, or weavers— two 6 inches long, two 5 inches long, and two 3 inches long. Weave as shown. On the back of the heart, paste the tops of the weavers in place.

Paste white hearts, about ½ inch across, on the ends of the weavers, as illustrated.

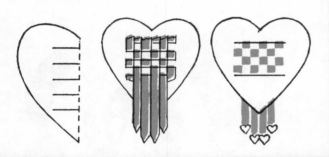

A Lacy Valentine

By Ilona Pinzke

Fold a piece of colored paper in half. Draw half a heart on the fold and cut it out.

Leave the heart folded. Use a paper punch to cut out a design inside the edge and through the center.

Open the heart. Weave colored paper ribbon through the design along the outside. Finish with a bow.

Make valentines out of red and white construction paper. Decorate them with candy hearts. Use a paste of powdered sugar and water to hold the candies in place so they can be eaten later. Write a valentine message on the front with crayon. Mount the valentines on contrasting construction paper or on a lace-paper doily cut a little larger than the decorated heart.

Here are a few ideas to try. Then think up some original ones.

Valentine Face

Use two hearts for eyes, one for a nose, and three for a mouth.

Valentine Notes

Draw the staff with red pencil across a white heart. Paste heart notes in different places on the staff. Finish the stems of the notes with crayon.

Valentine Arrows

Use a white pipe cleaner for the arrow. Insert it through two slits near the center of the heart. Use one candy heart for the tip of the arrow, and two for the end.

Ribbon Valentines

Paste candy hearts on four different lengths of pale-green ribbon and let dry. Cut a slit near the top of the valentine. Draw the top ends of the ribbon through to the back side and fasten them with cellophane tape. Paste a green ribbon bow at the top of the ribbons, using a candy heart for a center. Make a pink edging around the valentine before pasting it onto a larger heart.

Candy Heart Valentines

By Bernice Walz

Valentines should be gay and colorful. See how many ways
a heart shape can be used for all sorts of structures.
Hearts formed into containers for holding candy or flowers
are suggested here. Heart place cards and valentines to
send are also suggested. And, of course, the day would
not be complete without the valentine box covered with bows
of crepe paper and ribbon streamers.

basic pattern

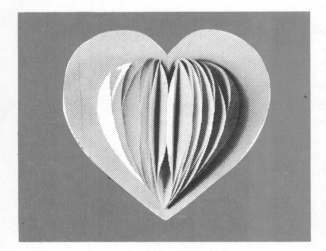

Cut eight or ten small hearts. Staple to larger heart,
bending each side forward in order to stand out.

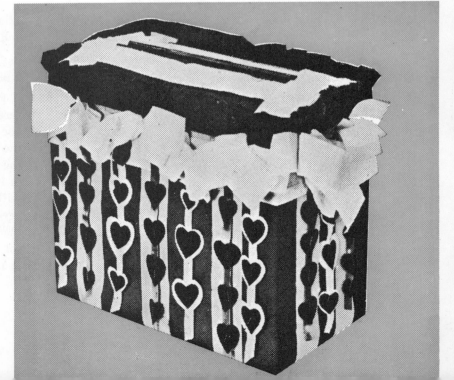

Adapted from "Creating With Paper" by Pauline Johnson,
published by the University of Washington Press,
Seattle, Washington.

Unusual Valentines

By Barbara Baker

Fold construction paper of different colors, and cut out hearts along the fold—some large, some small; some fat, some skinny. Cut and shape the hearts to make animals or people. Here are some ideas. Use your imagination to make more.

Mouse. Use a large red heart, upside down, for the body. Slit along the fold between the rounded ends. Insert and paste in place a long, pointed, curled tail. Crease the rounded ends forward, lapping and pasting them so the mouse will stand. Cut up from the bottom along the sides of the heart for arms. Cut ends for hands. Fold forward and attach a white heart with a message on it. The head is a white heart folded in half with the rounded ends bent forward for ears, and tiny red hearts for eyes.

Frog. Fold forward the rounded ends of a large heart for the frog's head. Pleat the rest of the heart. Paste two large white eyes with black centers on the face. Cut a narrow strip of paper the right length for the frog's legs. Fold the small pointed ends up for feet, then fold the rest to make a tent. Paste the legs to the heart on an upgoing fold. Attach narrow pointed strips for front legs, and bend them back. Paste to the hands a white heart with a valentine message.

Cat. The body is a long, skinny heart, upside down. Pleat it from tip to rounded ends, which bend forward for the front feet. The hind legs and feet are two hearts cut in half along the fold, pasted

together and then to the body as shown. Paste a long, pointed tail to the back. The head is two halves of a white heart, slashed for whiskers, and black-heart eyes. Ears are red hearts, slit up the fold, lapped and pasted in place.

Funny Face. Use a long heart, upside down. On the fold, cut a large, curved slit for the mouth, and another curved slit for the nose, pinching the crease to make it stand out. Add black fringed eyebrows, hair, and a heart-shaped derby hat. Paste on long, pointed arms. Attach hands, and bend to the back of the body where they hold a white-heart message. Bend rounded ends of heart forward for feet.

Clown. Long, narrow black hearts cut in half make arms and large feet for the clown. The body is a long, narrow pleated red heart. The head is a fat white heart with sides fringed for hair. Eyes are tiny black half hearts with a hole punched in the center of each. The tongue is made by bringing the pointed end of his body through a slit in his face. The hat is fastened in the center so the front edge may be folded up for a brim. Add a white triangular heart necktie with a printed message.

Valentine Day

49

A Crown for Valentine Day

By Ella L. Langenberg

Cut a crown pattern from newspaper. Measure a strip to go around the head, with a little extra to overlap. Fold it in the center and cut the points.

Trace the pattern on cardboard or heavy colored construction paper. Use as it is, or paint it with gold paint.

From scrap paper, cut heart patterns the right shape and size to fit the crown. Then cut the hearts from red construction paper.

Fasten each heart to a red or white pipe cleaner with gummed tape, then tape the pipe cleaners to the inner side of the crown.

Place the center heart highest and balance the other hearts on each side of it. They may also be placed in a row or in any other arrangement desired.

Chewing Gum Valentine

By Ellen E. Morrison

Cut a valentine heart about 5 inches wide from construction paper. In the center, cut two slots at a slant, about 1 inch long and ½ inch apart. Slip a stick of gum, with the wrapper on, through the slots. Put a small strip of gummed tape on the back side to hold the gum in place. Then letter this message on the front side of the valentine:

I chews you for my Valentine

Potato Print Valentines   By Jennifer Meigs Sanderson

On a fold of paper, draw and cut out three heart patterns of different sizes, as illustrated.

Cut potatoes in half. Lay each heart pattern on the flat, cut surface and draw around it. With a paring knife, cut away the potato outside each design so as to leave a raised heart. For a heart outline, cut away the potato from the inside of the raised heart shape.

From pieces of potato, cut various other shapes—small circles, diamonds, triangles, teardrops, ovals, or straight-line shapes.

Cut valentine cards from colored construction paper, and plan the overall design of the card.

To print the design, coat the surface of the potato stamps with poster paint, using a paintbrush. Press each shape lightly in place. If different colors are used, be sure to wash the stamp in cold water and dry it thoroughly with a paper towel before putting on a new color.

Standing Valentine Doll
By Margaret Squires

This doll can be mailed as a valentine, or used as a party favor.

From heavy red construction paper cut out one large heart for the body and two small hearts for the feet.

For the head, make a small loop in the center of a pipe cleaner, leaving the ends outstretched for arms. Bend the ends slightly for hands. Center the loop over the top of the body heart and fasten the arms to the heart with gummed tape. Cut a small head from an old magazine, place it over the loop, and fasten in back with gummed tape.

For the legs, bend a pipe cleaner in half. Place the bend in the center of the large heart. Fasten with tape. Bend the leg ends about ¾ inch to form feet. Place a small heart on top of each foot and fasten on the wrong side with tape. Bend the legs about halfway down so the doll will stand alone.

Colonial Hat
By Lucile Rosencrans

Make a hat for a Washington's birthday party or celebration. Use drawing paper or a large grocery sack. Cut out a circle 12 inches in diameter. Cut a circle out of the center large enough to fit the head. This should leave a brim about 3 inches wide. Color or paint the brim blue on both sides. Fold it into a triangular shape as shown by the dotted lines, to make a three-cornered hat. Decorate the left side with a cherry design if desired.

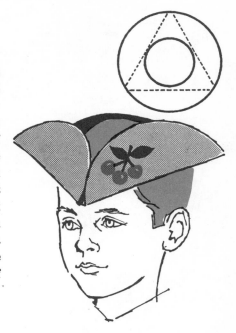

Pictures From Scraps
By Edna Ducote

It's fun to "build" a picture from scraps on hand. The illustrations show how easily it can be done. Both pictures were pasted on 9-by-12-inch blue construction paper.

The snow man, snowflakes, and clouds are white cotton. The hat and arms are black paper. The mouth and nose are red felt. The eyes are sequins.

The white-paper boy is fishing with a light-brown paper fishing pole. The boat is brown paper with pieces added to build up the front. The sky has white-cotton clouds with sequins and stars in the background. Water, fishline, and other lines were added with colored crayon.

Things To Do

Bunny Place Cards By Catherine Chase

For an Easter party, or for a surprise for the family, make a bunny place card for each person.

Fold a 3-by-5 inch card in half so it will stand up. Glue a large smooth-top button on the left side of the card, near the bottom, for the bunny's body. After the glue dries, put a small two-hole button above the large button and mark a dot with pen through each hole. Then glue the button in place for the head.

A half inch of ribbon makes the tie. Cut it in from the four corners to make a bow shape, and paste in place. Glue two pink paper ears to the card above the head. Add a red sequin for a hat. With red pencil, draw the mouth. With pen, draw on the facial features, feet, bow knot, and lines on the ears. Print the name with pen or colored pencil. A long name could be printed from the top down.

Eggshell Chick

By Barbara Baker

The body is half an eggshell. Push a plastic fork through a crack in the shell. Tape the fork to the inside of the shell. Fold a pipe cleaner in half and tape it to the bottom of the shell for legs. Tape the pipe-cleaner feet to a jar top so the chick will stand. Then use colored gummed paper, felt, feathers, or anything handy for the tail feathers and comb. Trim the neck with colored feathers, too, and stick a big one over his hindquarters to cover the hole in the shell. The eyes are a paper fastener but could be beads, sequins, or the like. The bill is a tiny folded piece of yellow gummed paper.

Flowers From Coins

By Judith L. LaDez

Place half dollars, quarters, nickels, pennies, and dimes in arrangements to suggest flowers, or any other designs. Draw around them in pencil. Decorate with colored pencils, crayons, or paint.

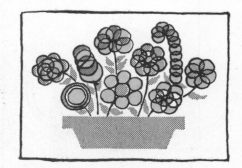

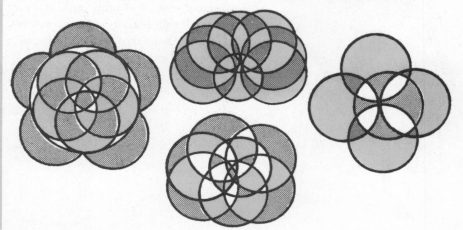

Many-colored Eggs

By Alice Stephen Gifford

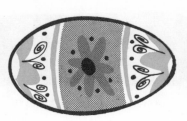

Here is a way to make Easter eggs with many colors on one egg, and with many designs.

Prepare some hard-boiled, white-shelled eggs, at least three different cups of egg coloring, and a piece of paraffin sharpened to a point.

To color the eggs in many colors, think about the design backwards. Instead of painting colors on, the design will be empty spaces where color will show through.

First, pick a basic color. It must be the lightest color to be used. If white is chosen, start drawing on the uncolored egg. If a light color like yellow is chosen, dip the egg into the yellow dye and let it dry.

Decide what is to stay yellow in the final design—perhaps some flowers and a little chick, with a big flower all over the top of the egg. Outline these designs on the dry egg and cover them completely with the paraffin stick.

Dip the egg in dye that is a little darker than the yellow—blue, perhaps. Let the egg dry. Now you will have a blue-green egg with yellow flowers and chick. They stayed yellow because no dye could get through the paraffin.

Next, draw some stems and grass and wavy lines with the paraffin stick. Dip the egg into another cup of dye, perhaps red. When the egg dries, there will be yellow flowers and chick, blue-green grass, stems, and wavy lines, and a red background.

The next part of the design will remain red when drawn with the paraffin, and so on till all the dyes are used.

Orange-can Totem Poles

By Joyce T. Buckner

This totem pole is made from three frozen orange juice cans, covered with papier-mâché. The following recipe will make enough for ONE can. Tear about three-fourths of a page of newspaper into bits about the size of a dime. Cover with hot water. Let stand about thirty minutes. Squeeze through the fingers till the mixture is mushy. There still should be a small amount of water in the bottom of the bowl. Sift flour over the mixture till it is all covered. Continue to squeeze through the fingers until all the water is absorbed.

Cover one of the cans with a thin layer of the papier-mâché, leaving about a half inch uncovered at the open end of the can. This can will be the bottom figure of the totem pole, with the open end of the can up. With the remaining mâché, make a nose and other facial features.

For the second can, make another batch of mâché. Apply to the can, leaving about a half inch uncovered at both the top and bottom.

On the top can, tape a sucker or ice-cream stick across the closed end of the can so it extends equally at the sides. Cover the can and stick with mâché, making a winged effect over the stick.

When the mâché is completely dry (it will take several days), pile the cans on top of one another. If they fall over, weight the bottom can with several stones and add wadded newspaper so the stones will not fall out. Tape the cans together with masking tape and cover it with mâché. This batch will take only about a fourth of a page of newspaper.

When dry, paint the totem pole with brown paint to look like wood. When this paint is dry, decorate the faces and wings in gay colors.

Bunny Basket
By M. Mable Lunz

Put four white or colored marshmallows together flat on the table. Put a long pipe cleaner around the outside, and twist the ends tight to hold the marshmallows firmly together. Clip off any extra ends. Bend another pipe cleaner and fasten it to the first cleaner at the sides, as shown, to form the handle.

Stick two toothpicks into the bottom of a candy rabbit, and stick the rabbit into the marshmallows.

A Box for Jewels
By Ella L. Langenberg

This jewel box is a handsome gift and easy to make.

First get a hinged box such as a cigar box. Paint the edges and the inside with gold paint.

Draw a line a quarter of an inch in from the edges of the sides and the top.

Cut colored magazine paper into strips, squares, and triangles. Paste them on the top and on all four sides of the box. Be careful to keep the paper even along the quarter-inch line.

Finish with one or two coats of clear shellac. To keep the brush soft, clean it in shellac thinner.

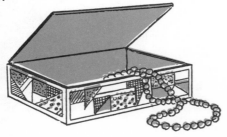

Make Your Own Easter Basket
By Mary Collette Spees

Cut out the pattern shown. Draw around the pattern on a 9-by-12-inch sheet of construction paper and cut out along the solid lines. Set aside the narrow strip at the edge to be used for a handle. Crayon or pencil eyes, nose, and whiskers on the rabbit face.

Fold up the sides and ends of the basket on the dotted lines. Paste together the ends marked A, then the ends marked B. This makes a little box. Fold up the head, and paste. Fold up the tail, and paste. Paste a cotton ball to the tail. Paste each end of the handle to the side of the basket.

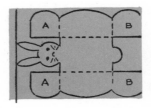

Ducky Nest
By M. Mable Lunz

Cut two ducks like the pattern, using white or yellow construction paper. Outline the eyes, bill, and wings with black crayon. Color the eyes green and the bill orange. Paste or glue the two heads together. Fold up the feet on the dotted line.

Paint a small paper plate with water colors or leave it white. Paste the ducks' feet to the bottom of the plate. Fill the sides of the plate with paper grass and jelly eggs. Put a colored hard-boiled Easter egg between the ducks for an extra surprise.

Easter Basket Decorations

By Clare Willis Ritter

Cut cardboard into Easter shapes—chickens, eggs, baskets, bunny rabbits.

Put 1 cup of detergent and ¼ cup of liquid plastic starch into a mixing bowl. Beat with a beater until it looks like thick marshmallow. Spread the mixture onto the cardboard cutouts. Let it stand about ten minutes, then dress up the cutouts. Use buttons for eyes, thread to outline bunny ears, thimbles for noses or bills, pipe cleaners for wings, toothpicks for whiskers.

Let the decorations dry overnight. Tint them with water colors when completely dry.

Sugar Head Kids

By Bernice Walz

These cute little characters can be used for cake decorations, or for tray favors on desserts or hot chocolate.

Materials needed are cube sugar, white or colored marshmallows, birthday cake decorations or tiny candies, and candy wafers or mints. A paste made from powdered sugar and water will hold them together.

On one side of the sugar cube, make a face with colored pencil or crayon. Use the cake decorations or tiny candies for hair, hat, or earmuffs. Paste a flat wafer or mint on top of a marshmallow, for a collar, then paste the head in place.

Make some of the Sugar Head Kids shown here. Then make some original characters.

A Pop-up Card

By Agnes Choate Wonson

Using the patterns shown on the squared drawing, cut the rabbit and spring from colored construction paper. Paint or crayon the rabbit with pink nose, mouth, eyes, and earholes. Outline with black ink and make other lines illustrated. Ink in the hind feet on the long section, and accordion-pleat the strip so it will pop up. Paste the rabbit head to the end pleat.

From contrasting paper, 2½ by 12 inches, cut the card. Cut the corners to make a point at each end as shown. Fold the card up 2½ inches from the bottom and down 3¾ inches from the top. Write the message in black on the inside of the top fold, and shade the letters with pink.

Paste a wad of cotton in the middle of the center section. Paste the hind legs to the cotton. Fold the top and bottom flaps over the rabbit, and the card is ready to mail.

55

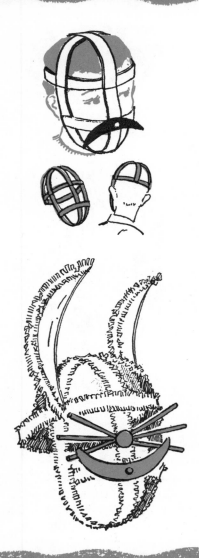

Rabbit With the Whirlabout Smile   By Virginia Follis

These masks may be worn at an Easter party, or used by actors in a play like "Peter Rabbit." The "smiles" may be turned upside down to look unhappy. Such masks may also be used for three-dimensional posters by flattening or cutting off the back parts of the mask. Different animal masks may be made by changing the shape of the ears and the color of the paper.

Use lightweight cardboard. A dress or suit box will do, or even a very large cereal box. Cut the box into long strips, at least an inch wide.

Build the mask over the head and face, strip by strip, removing it to paste or staple each strip in place as it is added. Be sure the mask is loose enough to go on and off easily.

Measure the first strip around the forehead, and paste. To this circle add a strip from front to back, and another from side to side, to form a beanie.

Add a strip running under the chin and up to the sides of the beanie; and another from under the chin, up over the mouth and nose, to the beanie. The last strip goes across the mouth to the sides of the mask.

Paste double strips of fringed white crepe paper over the cardboard strips. If staples are used, be sure they are well covered inside the mask to protect the face.

Make the crescent-shaped ears from a 9-inch paper plate, cover with fringed crepe paper, and fasten securely in place. Whiskers can be made from colored pipe cleaners or sip straws, fastened under the red-circle nose.

Cut a crescent-shaped mouth from cardboard. Cover it with red paper. Punch a hole in the center and fasten to the mask with a two-pronged paper fastener.

Paper Easter Eggs   By Bernice Walz

Cut some egg shapes from white and colored construction paper. Cut apart old greeting cards to make pretty borders, flowers, and allover designs on the eggs. Edges and parts of gold doilies are especially pretty in carrying out a design.

These eggs can be used in several ways. Make an Easter egg tree by tying many eggs to a small tree branch which has been set in a pot of sand.

Or make a double-egg greeting card or party invitation, keeping one side joined. Write the message or invitation on the inside.

In whatever way they are used, these original creations will be sure to please.

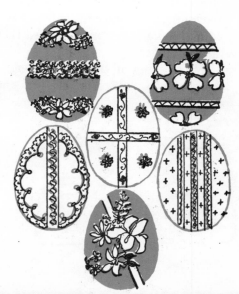

A Lily for Easter

By Ella L. Langenberg

Cut white tablet paper, 5 by 9 inches. Fold it in half to 5 by 4½ inches. Mark the corners as in Figure 1. The dotted lines always indicate a folded edge.

Fold the bottoms, A-B, over to A-X, and crease, as in Figure 2. Then fold the A-X edge back under to the A-C edge, and crease, as in Figure 3. Cut along the heavy lines shown in Figure 3.

Open the paper, and cut off the shaded parts shown in Figure 4. Be careful not to cut off the section marked "for pasting."

With the scissors blade, curl the points. These are the petals of the lily.

Before pasting the flower, wrap a piece of yellow crepe paper over the end of a stick or long pipe cleaner. Tie it with thread. Fold the lily around the stem, far enough down so the yellow center shows as pictured. Paste and tie the lily to the stem.

Cut green leaves from construction paper. Paste them to the stem as shown.

Wind a long, narrow strip of green crepe paper around the stem, covering the ends of the leaves, too.

Plant the lily in a wax paper cup. Put enough heavy soil in the cup to hold the lily in place.

Wrap aluminum foil around the cup. Put a colored ribbon around it, and tie in a pretty bow.

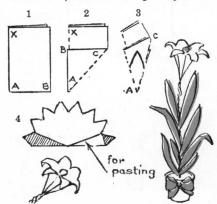

Easter Eggs

By Betsy Jane Boyd

These Easter eggheads are easy to make and fun to experiment with. Make boys and girls, bunnies, outer-space people, favorite story characters. For the Easter dinner, make one to represent each member of the family as a place favor. Add one to an Easter basket as a finishing touch.

Use blown eggs for the heads, strands from a metallic scouring pad for hair, fringed plastic ribbon for eyelashes, sequins or bits of plastic ribbon for features. For hats and collars, use bits of lace-paper doilies, colored fluted baking cups, or empty ribbon spools. Trim with artificial flowers or bits of ribbon.

Paste everything in place with colorless glue or cement. It dries quickly and won't show.

After Easter, save the favorite eggheads and keep them on a whatnot or in a shadow box. Each egghead needs a stand to support the round-bottomed eggshell—such as a paper nut cup, empty ring-shaped ribbon spool, or a circle of pipe cleaner with legs attached as shown.

Easter Basket

By Cecille B. Bowmann

Draw and cut out the basket shape shown, about 5½ inches high and 4 inches wide. Place it on a fold of heavy colored construction paper, with the handle end on the fold, and cut out. Cut V-shaped slits on each side as shown by the heavy line. Each side of the V should be about 2 inches long. Cut out and discard the shaded areas.

For the bottom of the basket, cut a 3½-inch square of paper from a contrasting color. Fold it in half, crease, open, and run through the V-shaped slits. Spread the basket sides over the bottom piece. Fill with paper grass and candy Easter eggs.

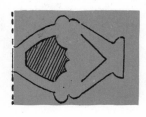 

57

For the Birds

When cold winds blow and snow covers the ground, birds have a hard time finding enough food to eat. Here are some easy bird feeders that can be made to help them out.

Breakfast for the Birds
By Lois Kauffman

Use the skin from half a grapefruit. Mix softened suet with cracked wheat and cooky crumbs. Place this mixture in the grapefruit skin to harden. Punch two tiny holes on opposite sides of the grapefruit and run a string through them for a handle to hang on a branch.

Or fill an empty soup can with the mixture used for the grapefruit, adding weed seeds and anything else that birds like. When it has hardened, cut out the bottom of the can. Run a stick through the suet to serve as a perch. Punch a hole at each end of the can, and run a wire through to form a hanger, as shown.

Swinging Bird Feeders   By Anobel Armour

Use little foil plates that frozen pies come in.

Punch a hole in one side of the plate, and another on the opposite side. Cut a 10-inch piece of heavy cord. Make a knot in one end. Run the cord through one of the holes, with the knot underneath. Then push the cord down through the other hole and knot it. The cord should loop up and be about 8 inches long.

Fasten another cord in the same way to the other two opposite sides of the plate. Fasten them together where they cross.

Fill the plate with bread crumbs, cracker crumbs, or seeds.

These swinging bird feeders can be put anywhere. They could even be carried a little way into the woodland and hung on the trees there, if the winter happens to be an especially hard one for birds. And they cost little or nothing.

Peanut Butter Feeder   By Lawry Turpin

Birds like peanut butter. A fine way to serve it to them is to use a piece of thick wood about 1¾ inches square and 1 foot long.

Just draw a line down the center of two opposite sides and put dots on it 3½ inches and 8½ inches down from the top. On the other two sides put the dots 1½ inches and 6 inches down from the top. In each one of these bore a hole 1 inch in diameter and about ¾ inch deep.

Place the perches 1½ inches below each large hole. Their diameter should be that of a meat skewer or a very small dowel. Cut the perches 2 inches long. Glue them in place.

Fasten a screw eye in the center of the top for a hanging wire. Stain green or brown.

Leave the feeder outdoors for two or three days until the stain smell is all gone. Then pack each large hole with peanut butter and hang it up.

Now sit back and watch the chickadees and the nuthatches find the feeders. Listen for their "chick-a-dee-dee-dees" and "ank-anks" which say "thank you."

Soon the hairy and downy woodpeckers will fly up and sample the food. Juncos are sure to pay a visit—and cardinals, too, if you are lucky. Even a saucy blue jay will snatch a bite when he thinks no one is looking.

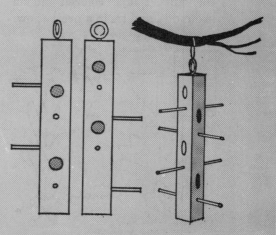

Let's Make a Mobile

By Thomas P. Ramirez

This easy-to-make mobile has no required design. It's like little Topsy—it just grows.

Materials needed are eight or ten sticks of balsa, ⅛ by ⅛ by 36 inches, a tube of model cement, several sheets of tissue paper of different colors, some straight pins, a single-edge razor blade, a piece of stiff flat cardboard, some waxed paper, and a spool of dark thread.

Cut and glue the balsa sticks in interesting patterns as in Figure 1. Choose shapes and patterns which appeal to you. Put wax paper over the cardboard to keep the glue from sticking to the cardboard. Pin the pieces to the cardboard. Glue and trim the balsa wood at each joint.

You should make one main geometrical shape upon which the rest of the construction will be mounted. This main shape should be larger than the other parts. Don't be afraid to experiment with odd shapes.

Make several smaller shapes to use for danglers. If your designs lie flat on the table, they have just TWO DIMENSIONS. You can make them in THREE DIMENSIONS by attaching some of the pieces so that they point up from the table, like a pyramid or a cube.

Choose the areas which you think will look best covered with tissue. Try to choose colors which look well together. Before you cover, brace large areas with balsa sticks to make them more rigid.

Spread glue on the balsa sticks of the area to be covered, and apply the tissue. Be sure no part of the paper is left unfastened. Neatly trim off excess tissue with your razor blade.

When the glue is dry, dampen the tissue paper. When the paper dries, it will shrink and draw tight, giving a neat finished job.

You may want to use other materials to add special effects to your designs. Wire, yarn, aluminum foil, window screening, and many other common materials can be quite interesting.

Now you are ready to hang the pieces together to make a mobile. The secret of an attractive mobile is that parts hang from one another in interesting ways, and swing about in balance in the air.

The mobile in Figure 2 looks very plain and regular. In Figure 3 it looks much more alive and interesting.

You will find that you can most easily balance your mobile if you start with the bottom danglers and build upward. Fasten the thread with a small spot of glue, or tie it. Be careful not to make the thread too long for it will spoil the unity of your mobile.

Hang your mobile from the ceiling and watch what interest it will arouse among your family and friends.

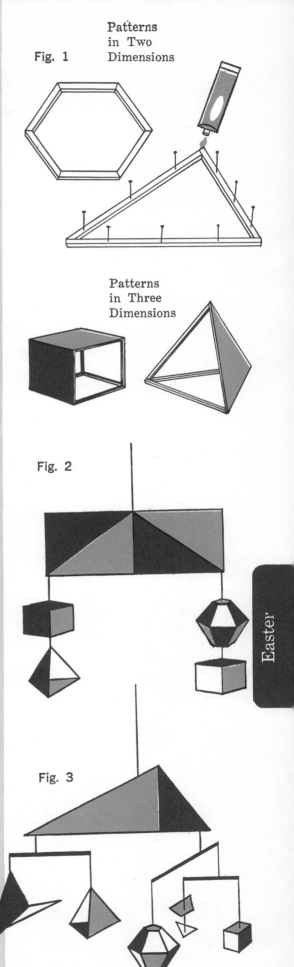

Fig. 1 — Patterns in Two Dimensions

Patterns in Three Dimensions

Fig. 2

Fig. 3

Easter

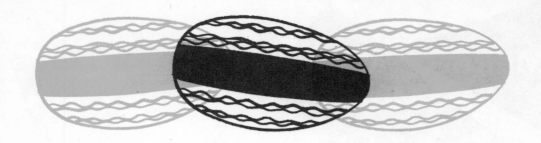

Handkerchief Bunny
By Barr Clay Bullock

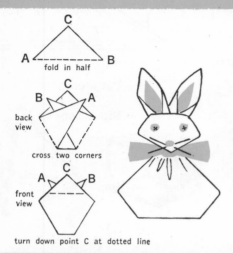

C

A — — — — B

fold in half

back view

B   C   A

cross two corners

front view

A   C   B

turn down point C at dotted line

Fold a man's white handkerchief in half, diagonally. Follow the illustrations for the arrangement of the two corners for ears, and the turned-down corner for the face. Sew on pink buttons for eyes, 2-inch brown straws for the X-shaped whiskers, and a little pink construction paper mouth. Paste a pink paper oval in each ear corner. Gather the handkerchief under the face, and tie with a bright ribbon bow. Pin up the bottom of the handkerchief so the bunny will look fat and chubby.

Place the bunny at Dad's place at the breakfast table for a surprise Easter gift.

Gay Tulips
By Barr Clay Bullock

Use an egg carton with rounded egg cups. Cut out each cup, trimming the pointed corners. Paint the cups with different colors to look like tulip blossoms.

Punch a tiny hole in the bottom of each cup. Stick a pipe-cleaner stem through the hole. Inside the cup, let the stem stick up about a half inch. Wrap a tiny wisp of cotton on the end, and paint it yellow.

Cut tulip leaves from green construction paper and attach to the stems with gummed tape. Stick the stems into a spiked flower holder or a small vase for a pretty Easter flower arrangement.

Puppet
By Evelyn Walker

Use a wooden picnic spoon. Make eyes and mouth with paint or crayons. Paste cotton on back and around edges for hair. Make a simple dress by wrapping a piece of colored cloth around it, holding it on with a piece of pipe cleaner.

An Easter Hello
By Carol Conner

For the card, cut a 6-by-9-inch piece of heavy white or light-colored construction paper. Fold in half to 6 by 4½ inches.

On smooth white paper, draw several small eggs. Decorate with gay poster paints or colored inks.

Draw a 1-inch tab on one egg as shown. Decorate this egg so it stands out from the others, using a single dark color, or gold and silver paint. Write the sender's name on the tab.

Cut out the eggs and paste them over each other as shown. Then paste them inside the folder, leaving an unpasted space in which to slip the tabbed egg.

Spread paste on the nest area. Cover it with a long strip of ⅛-inch crepe paper, crumpling and curling it back and forth. Press it down, adding dabs of paste to hold the curls in place.

Seal the folder with an Easter seal or one of the decorated eggs. Put the address and postage on the outside of the folder.

Nut Cup
By Ann Hatch

Let a white eggshell dry for several days. Remove the thin skin. Crush the shell with a rolling pin until it is in fairly fine pieces, but not powdery.

Mix white poster paint with paste to give it a nice white color. Add a little water if necessary, until the mixture is like a thick starch.

Cut two strips of colored construction paper about ¾ inch wide. Staple the ends to the sides of a 3-inch colored paper cup to form a handle. The two strips make a stronger handle.

Using the white paste, paint a design on the cup. Sprinkle the crushed eggshell over the design. The eggshell will stick to the white paste, giving the design a delicate, lacy look.

Egg Doll
By Ruth E. Libbey

Paint a smiling face and hair on one side of a blown-out eggshell.

For the bonnet, fold a paper muffin cup almost in half. Place a piece of colored ribbon or yarn in the fold. The ends will be the bonnet strings. Tie the bonnet on the eggshell head.

For the body, use a 4½-inch length of cardboard tubing. Or roll cardboard and slip rubber bands over each end to hold in place. Cut out the centers of four or five colored paper muffin cups. Slip the fluted edges over the roll, and tape in place. Place the head on top. Make a doll favor for each place at the Easter Day meal.

For Mother's Day

Baskets   By Bernice Walz

Trim the rim from the edge of an individual foil pie tin. Cut fringe about an inch deep around the tin. Punch a hole on opposite sides of the bottom of the tin. Stick a 6-inch colored or white pipe cleaner through each hole, bending the ends over to hold them securely. Twist the other ends together to form a handle. Finish with a colored ribbon bow.

Use two colored crinkly baking cups, one pasted inside the other, for the basket. Paste them with rubber .cement to the center of the pie tin. Fill with small candies and popcorn.

Candles

By Miriam Lister

Collect old candles and candle ends. Melt them in a coffee can over water. An older person should help, as the wax becomes very hot and is dangerous to handle.

Paint varied sizes of bottle caps with colorful enamel, and set them aside to dry. Take a piece of wick from one of the candles. Glue one end to the bottom center of a bottle cap. Fill the cap with the melted wax and allow it to cool. Cut off the wick slightly above the wax.

Mother will enjoy these little lighted candles among the floating blossoms in her centerpiece.

Hand Plaque   By Stella Matthews

Any mother would be delighted with this gift—a print of baby's hand or foot.

Place an embroidery hoop or a picture frame on a sheet of heavy paper or cardboard. Mix equal amounts of plaster of Paris and water until it will spread nicely. Fill the hoop or frame with this mixture.

Cover baby's hand with vaseline. Press it firmly into the plaster. Lift it out carefully so the impression will not be blurred.

Before the plaster sets firmly, pierce it at the top with a large needle to make a hole for a hanger. Let the plaque dry thoroughly.

Mix water-color paint of the desired color. Drop it on the handprint and spread carefully over the handprint with the fingers. Then outline the print with a contrasting color. When the paint is thoroughly dry, brush on a coat of shellac to seal it. Let dry thoroughly. Use a ribbon or cord for hanging.

This makes a beautiful and lasting gift for anyone who loves the baby.

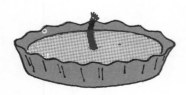

Hat Stand

By Frances Benson

A round oatmeal box can be made into a pretty stand for a girl's hat. A good-sized rock or several small ones should be put inside, to weigh it down. Glue or tape on the lid. Cover the box with colored wrapping paper or construction paper. Decorate the stand with a ribbon bow or a picture cut from a magazine.

Plant   By Ruth Dougherty

Cut a 24-inch length of corrugated paper, 2½ inches wide; and a 6-inch length, 1 inch wide.

To form the flowerpot, roll the wide strip into a solid cylinder, smooth side out. Strip off one row of the corrugated paper at the end to leave a flat lap for gluing. Hold in place with a rubber band until dry.

Glue the 1-inch strip to the top of the pot for a rim, corrugated side out. Paint the pot inside, then outside.

For the flowers, make a pattern by cutting four scallops around a 1-inch square of paper. Trace around the pattern on colored construction paper. Cut out four of these scalloped petals for each flower. Make holes in centers, and slip onto green pipe cleaner stems. On top of the last scalloped petal, slip a tiny circle of yellow paper.

Cut three long, green paper leaves. Make holes in the ends and slip them up onto the stem.

Make several flowers and stand them in the holes formed by the corrugated paper of the flowerpot.

Covered Jewelry Box

By M. Mable Lunz

Use a small box about an inch deep such as a half-pound candy box. Slit two corners of the box cover, Figure 1.

Lay the cover upside down on a piece of pretty material. Cut the material large enough to bring up over the sides, with an extra half inch inside the cover, all around.

Bring the material over the front and sides, Figure 2, folding it at the outside corners carefully. Put gummed tape along the inside to hold the material in place.

Put the cover on the box. Punch two holes through the back edge of the cover and of the box. Put a two-pronged paper fastener through each hole from the inside of the box and spread it open at the back. Or run a long piece of double string through the holes and tie it in back.

Cut out the back corners of the material to fit. Fold it over the back of the cover and down under the box bottom. Glue in place.

Trim the cover with initials cut from a different color material, or make a design from odd pieces. Glue in place.

Fig. 1

Fig. 2

May Baskets

A Gift for Mother
By Ella L. Langenberg

Paste a circle of purple construction paper to the center of a lace-paper doily. Fold this in half to form a basket.

Cut flower shapes from pink and yellow construction paper. These may be cut freehand or on a fold of paper as shown. Cut leaves and stems from green paper. Paste the flowers to the stems, then to the basket, as shown.

Fold the basket and paste the two sides together. Punch a hole at the top of the basket. Put a ribbon through it and finish with a bow.

Umbrella Basket
By Jinx Woolson

Fold an 8-inch circle of colored construction paper into sixteen equal sections. Number the sections clockwise as shown. On the other side of the circle, paste an 8-inch lace-paper doily for the outside of the basket.

Fold sections 1 and 2 with the outsides together. Lay section 2 against section 10. Staple the three sections together.

Fold sections 13 and 14, outsides together, and staple. Do the same with sections 5 and 6.

For the handle, cut a strip of paper 9 inches long and ½ inch wide. Loop the strip. Fasten the ends between sections 15 and 3, toward the back of the basket for easier hanging on the doorknob.

Make a yellow paper daffodil and attach for decoration.

Cooky Basket
By Erma Reynolds

A small white or pastel lace-paper doily forms the bottom of the basket. Place a teacup on a piece of foil paper. Mark around it with pencil. Cut out this circle, using pinking scissors if possible, and lay it on the lace doily.

Cut four slits as shown, so they will come in exactly the same place on the foil and the doily.

Using light-colored construction paper, cut two strips 11 inches long and ¾ inch wide. Run them through the slits in the foil and doily as shown. Bring the four ends together over the basket. Staple or sew them with coarse white thread. Do not pull the stitches too tight or the paper will tear. Cut out a small picture of flowers from an old greeting card or magazine and paste it on the handle to hide the staple or stitches. Place two or three small round cookies on the foil.

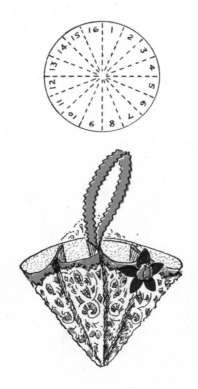

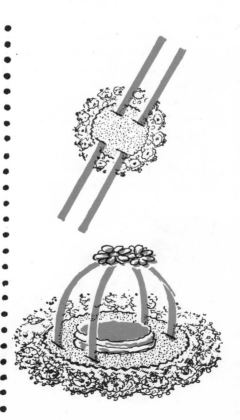

A Crayon Bucket

By Antoinette Bosco

Cut a round cereal box down to a 5-inch height. Use a ruler to mark the box so it will be the same height all around.

Paint the box and the cover, or paste pictures on them. Let them dry.

Punch a hole 1 inch down on opposite sides of the box, and on opposite sides of the cover near the edge.

Run some twine or ribbon through the holes in the bucket and the cover to make a handle, as illustrated.

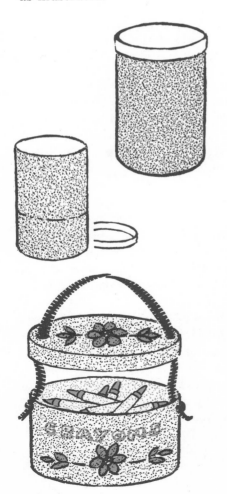

Texture Pictures

By Virginia Appelt

To make a texture picture, use real objects instead of paints or crayons. A house is made of real wood, the stones on a path are real stones, a bird is made of real feathers, and so on.

Make the picture on a shallow box lid or a piece of heavy paper. It's a good idea to sketch in the objects with a pencil first. Then spread glue on each place where the object will be, and start building the picture by placing bits of material on the glue.

Use twigs for trees and fences, stones for paths and walls, dried grass and flowers for gardens. Cotton makes good fur for animals. All sorts of seeds can be used for a background. Bits of cloth make real clothes for the people in the picture.

Many other materials can be used to make these interesting texture pictures as they are being "painted."

Polka-dot and Checkered Stationery

By Agnes Choate Wonson

Mother's scrapbag will offer many bright-colored gingham and cotton-print scraps which can be used in decorating note paper. Girls would like the flower design. Boys would probably prefer the sailboats.

In the suggestions shown, the flower blossoms and the triangular sails were cut from cloth and pasted (not glued) on colored note paper. The wave-lines and gulls, the stems and ferny leaves, may be done in crayon or water color.

A box of note paper makes a nice gift, especially with decorated sheets and envelopes to fit.

Mother's Day

65

By Gertrude Springer

Make the clay from 2 cups of coarse salt, 1 cup of boiling water, and 1 cup of cornstarch. Boil the salt and water. Put the cornstarch in another dish and slowly stir in cold water until it will pour. Add it to the boiling mixture. Keep stirring till it is very thick and transparent. Pour it out on wax paper to cool.

Divide the clay. Color the different sections with cake coloring, leaving one part white. Roll the clay flat with an olive bottle. Cover a bottle or can with it. Pinch out petals and leaves or other shapes from colored clay, and add designs.

Cover metal book ends with plain-colored clay. From brown clay, cut and vein leaves, using real leaves for patterns. Press them on the book ends. Add acorns to finish the decoration.

Shape doll dishes, such as cups and saucers. Roll a bit of colored clay for the handles. Trim the dishes with designs of colored clay. Let dry for a few days, pressing out any cracks that appear.

Keep the leftover clay in wax paper in the refrigerator.

Fun With Scraps

By Evelyn White Minshull

Here are some games that everyone will enjoy. Make up a kit of different-colored pieces of construction paper for each player. Each kit should have two each of some of the shapes, alike in size and color, to use for eyes, ears, and the like. These kits may be used for several games at the same party.

Pass out sheets of paper on which a head shape and neck ruffle are already drawn. See who can create, most quickly and skillfully, a happy clown or a sad one.

Or suggest that each player create a picture, using as many pieces as possible, and adding picture details with crayon. These could be pasted to a sheet of construction paper and displayed on the wall, to be judged by the guests.

Or give the players 9-by-12-inch sheets of paper. Then, with only a little time allotted to each picture creation, assign topics, and watch the players scramble to assemble their pictures. Some topic suggestions are Christmas tree, lollipop, balloon on a string, tall house and small house, house by the side of the road, mailbox, umbrella, tepee at night.

Frame for Snapshots
By Margaret Olson

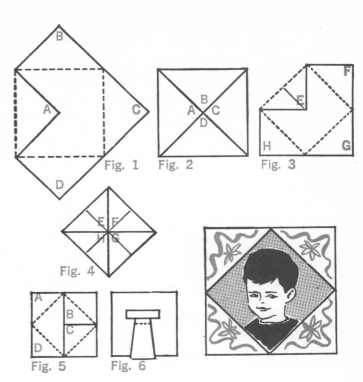

Fig. 1 Fig. 2 Fig. 3
Fig. 4
Fig. 5 Fig. 6

Cut a piece of construction paper 7 or 9 inches square. Fold corners A, B, C, and D in toward the center on the dotted lines, as in Figure 1. The paper now looks like Figure 2.

Turn this square over with the topside down. Fold corners E, F, G, and H toward the center on the dotted lines, Figure 3. It will look like Figure 4.

Fasten down corners E, F, G, and H with transparent gummed tape. Turn the square over so the other side is again on top.

Fold points A, B, C, D up and back to the edge, to form the frame, Figure 5.

Decorate these flaps if desired. Slip the snapshot under the flaps.

To hang the picture, tape a loop of string on the back. If the frame is to stand up, fasten a cardboard strip to the back, creasing it as in Figure 6.

Carnation Coaster
By Agnes Choate Wonson

A set of pink or red carnation coasters is a nice gift sure to please Mother.

Make a pattern for the curving stem and leaf as shown. Cut from green construction paper. Cut the flower from crepe paper. Place the flower under the end of the stem. Put between two pieces of wax paper and press gently with a warm iron. Using a cup, trace around the flower, and cut it out.

Hot Dish Mat
By Joyce A. Sutherland

Cut a square or circle from an old corrugated cardboard box. With black crayon, make a scribble picture on both sides. Use other colors to fill in between the scribbles. Be sure to color all the cardboard. Put adhesive or bookbinding tape around the edges. Cover both sides with three coats of clear shellac. This will make the mat shine, and will help to make it heatproof.

Cutout Paper Fans
By Judith L. LaDez

Start with a sheet of paper about 8½ by 11 inches. Accordion-pleat it with each pleat about ¾ inch wide. Cut designs along the edges about halfway down the strip. Turn up the bottom as shown, and staple or tape it together for a neat finish.

Making these would be good fun at parties, with the maker of the most beautiful fan winning the prize.

Elephant Hand Puppet
By Phyllis Fanders

This is fun to make and easy to use. It is made from a paper bag which has a square bottom. Trunk, ears, and tusks are cut from heavy paper and pasted to the sack. Everything is colored or painted except the tusks.

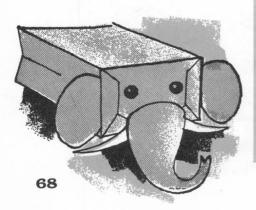

Paper Cup Mule
By Barbara Baker

Four paper drinking cups make this mule. One cup is his head. Cut one in half for his neck, turn it upside down and use a paper fastener on each side to hitch it to his head. Cut two ears from the other cup half. Slit two holes in the top of the head, and insert the ears.

His tummy is another whole cup. Cut around half of the bottom, fold it down, and staple it to the bottom of his neck. Now his head can wag up and down.

His legs are one cup cut in half with a V cut up the middle of each half. Fasten each half under his tummy with a paper fastener. Push two pipe cleaners with beads on the ends through the bottom of the neck section and out for the tail. Hold the tail ends in place with the prong ends of a paper fastener. When you pull them back and forth, he can almost "hee-haw." The felt-circle eyes are held in place with paper fasteners. A piece of colored yarn makes the mouth.

Put clay on his feet if you want him to stand.

A Lacy Basket
By Ruth Everding Libbey

Use a paper lunch dish for this basket, or a drinking cup for a taller basket. Turn it upside down on top of a small lace-paper doily. Trace around it with pencil. Then cut out the center of the doily, about ½ inch in from the tracing line. Cut little slits around the hole to the tracing line.

Dab glue all the way around the cup near the top. Pull the doily up over the cup. Let the slit pieces dry in the glue. Cover them with ribbon or rickrack, gluing it in place. Decorate the bottom of the cup in the same way.

Punch a hole on each side of the cup and insert a pipe-cleaner handle, bending the ends to hold it in place.

68

Do

Cards for Mother's Day
By Beatrice Bachrach

Fold a sheet of construction paper in half for the greeting card. Scallop the bottom of the front half as shown. Draw, cut out, and paste colored flowers on the front. Metallic paper gives the card extra glitter. Add stems and leaves with crayon. Paste dabs of cotton in center of each flower. Sequins may be added if desired.

Paste a wide border of the same color as the flowers on the inside bottom of the back half. Write the message above it.

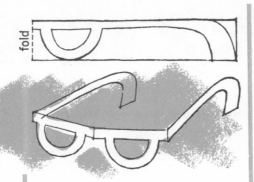

Cardboard Spectacles

Cut a strip of lightweight cardboard, 3 by 15 inches. Fold it in half, lengthwise. Cut a pair of spectacles as shown.

Experiment until you find the right size for your eyes.

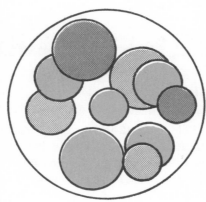

A Gift for Mother
By Ella L. Langenberg

Cut a cardboard circle or use those inside the tin cover on coffee, peanut butter, or other glass jars. Wash and dry the cardboard.

Trace around quarters, nickels, dimes, and pennies to make a design. Have some of the circles overlap. Fill in the circles with the colored crayons you like. Color the edge of the cardboard, too. Daddy will help you put a coat of shellac over the cardboard to make it waterproof.

Mother will be glad to get this coaster to protect the table top from water, coffee, tea, or other things that might drip or spill.

Make a Snake
By Dorothe A. Palms

Materials needed are a large-eyed needle threaded with a 30-inch-long string, a piece of white cardboard, 3 inches by 5 inches, and cardboard boxes from cake mixes, facial tissues, cereals, crackers, and the like.

Cut the boxes into 1-inch squares. Run the needle through the center of the squares, threading them on the string to the desired length. Then make a snake head like pattern, fold it on the dotted line, and thread it on last, through the square part only. Glue the string to the back of the snake head, leaving a piece of string sticking out past the mouth. Dip this string end into red ink.

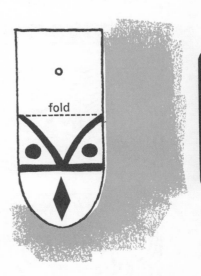

fold

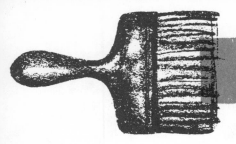

Reversible Snow Man

By Ruth Dougherty

Bend a white pipe cleaner into a circle for the body. Overlap the ends and tie with white thread. Cut a circle of heavy white paper for the head. On both sides, paste scraps of colored paper for eyes and mouth. Glue the head to the body where the pipe cleaner overlaps.

From black paper cut out two high hats. Paste them together, inserting the head between them before the paste dries.

Twist short pieces of pipe cleaner into place for arms. On a fold of colored paper cut two double mittens. Paste one over the end of each arm.

Make two red bows from pipe cleaners, felt, or paper. Glue them at the neck, front and back.

Stand the snow man in a small piece of clay, or run a thread hanger through the hat.

Glamour Glasses

By Marjorie Weed

Fold 4-by-12-inch colored construction paper to 4 by 6 inches. On it draw half of the nosepiece, and one lens and bow, with the nosepiece on the fold. At the top of the lens, draw horns or a fancy shape. Cut out the glasses and the center of the lenses. Unfold and decorate with sequins, glitter, or colored yarn.

Eyelashes may be cut at the top in place of trim, or may be made by cutting out the center of the lenses along the bottom and sides, fringing these centers, and folding them up over the lens tops.

This would make a good party game, with the best idea winning a prize.

Fun With Names

By Bernice Walz

With colored crayon, write a name slantwise across a piece of white construction paper. Using a different color, draw a line around the name, about 1/4 inch away. Continue doing this, using several different colors. Then repeat the colors in the same order as first used, until the paper is filled. The name may be left in outline, or the spaces may be colored in as the paper is filled.

This name design may be mounted on paper and hung on the wall. Or scrapbook covers may be made, using such words as ANIMALS, STAMPS, and the like.

Bark Centerpiece

By Barbara Baker

Find a piece of thick bark, or an old piece of wood full of knots and holes, with perhaps some moss on it. Paint the little knobs on it to look like little colored bugs with spots. Paint tiny acorns and caps, tiny pine cones, and little twigs to look like little men or birds or animals. Glue them in place.

Peanut Parrot

By L. Mary Doran

Use an unshelled peanut for the body.

Cut several pieces of crepe paper about 6 inches long and 1/4 inch wide. Use several different colors. Paste one end of each strip to the rounded end of the peanut. Cut out a pair of wings on a fold of green crepe paper, and paste to the body as shown. Insert a small stick in the bottom of the peanut. Push the other end of the stick into a clay base, or use a large gumdrop.

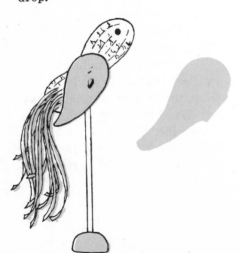

Wall Switch Cover

By Paul J. Bauer, Jr.

Draw and cut out a switch cover pattern in one piece. Trace it onto thin, very stiff cardboard. For a permanent decoration, use aluminum flashing, cutting it with tin shears. It will bend as it is cut, but is easily straightened. To cut out the middle areas, use a very sharp linoleum knife, or drill a hole to insert the scissors.

Straighten the edges and smooth the aluminum by laying it on a piece of hard wood, pressing firmly all around the cut edges with a smooth piece of wood such as the handle of a hammer or screw driver. Smooth off any sharp edges, points, or slivers with a nail file. Any scratches or gouges should be sanded firmly with #400 waterproof sandpaper covered with oil or water. Clean it off with turpentine.

Spray or paint the entire cutout, and the old switch cover, using flat or semi-gloss black paint. Spraying will give a much smoother finish.

To assemble, mount the cutout over the switch box, then put the old switch cover on top and fasten with the same screws.

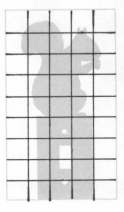

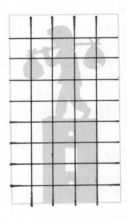

Each square represents one inch

Candy Train

By Woody Vick

Make the train from marshmallows, moistening the ends which are to be stuck together. Use candies with a hole in the center for wheels, and pieces of candy cane for smokestacks. Use small marshmallow for the caboose and the front of the train. Chocolate squares may be used for windows.

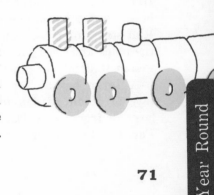

Year Round

Frisky Zoo Friends   By Texie Hering

Use half a walnut shell for each head. Make features with quick-drying white paint, black for eye centers. Trace around each shell on lightweight cardboard, and cut out. Paste to the back of the shell, inserting tan yarn ears or mane between cardboard and shell.

Cut 3-by-2-inch cages from bright-colored construction paper. Using a ruler, draw bars ¼ inch apart with brown crayon. Paste each head to a cage as shown. Paste or tape one end of a 3-inch yarn tail to the back of each cage. Shape the tail ends as shown.

Tape a looped-yarn hanger to the back of each cage.

Pony or Hippo   By Hilda K. Watkins

Cut about 2 inches off the bottom of a small cereal box. Cover it with paper from a large manila envelope. Clip on spring-type clothespins at each corner for legs. Cut and paste on a fringed paper tail.

At the bottom corner of the envelope, draw and cut out a horse's head as shown. Slit down the edge from the corner and fold out the points for ears.

Fold a strip of the manila paper, and cut a fringed mane and forelock. Paste them in place. Draw mouth, nostrils, and eyes. Run shoelace reins through holes at each corner of the mouth.

The two front clothespins will hold the head to the body.

For the hippopotamus, omit the mane and forelock, make smaller eyes, and flatten out the nose.

Round-handled Baskets   By Hilda K. Watkins

These baskets may be made from any size box desired. Place the hoop handle inside the box from corner to corner. Punch holes in the bottom of the box. Run string or ribbon up through the holes and over the handle, to fasten it firmly in place.

A large basket for carrying toys or small garden tools may be made from a cardboard carton. For the handle, use a wooden

hoop from the top of a peach basket. Tie this handle at the corners, too. Paint the entire basket, and the handle.

For sewing box size, use a small candy box or the bottom 3

inches of a cereal box, and an embroidery hoop handle. Cover the box with fancy paper. Wind ribbon around the handle.

To make the handle for the smallest basket, cut off ¼ inch from the top of a small paper cup. Wind this hoop with ribbon. Cover the box with aluminum foil. If the box is used for candy or nuts, line it with a tiny lace-paper doily.

Push-pull Dollhouse   By Virginia Follis

This house can be pulled apart to pack away, or to carry to a friend's house. Paper dolls may be carried in envelopes. Boys can make garages, stores, or fire stations, using this idea.

From a corrugated paper box, cut two pieces 12 by 19 inches. Cover them with wallpaper or gift paper on both sides. Wallpaper paste is best for this. Smooth out all wrinkles carefully. Weight the pieces down with books or magazines while they dry, so they will not warp.

When dry, mark the center of each piece on the 19-inch side, and cut a slit halfway down. Make the slit wide enough so the two pieces can be fitted together as shown. If they are not quite "square," wedge in a toothpick or small piece of cardboard to hold them straight.

Paste cloth curtains at the window. A paper fastener or a small bead makes a good doorknob. Cut pictures from old magazines and paste on the walls.

Use ready-made doll furniture, or paste cutouts from old magazines on boxes such as gelatin or matches come in. Cutouts can also be pasted on heavy paper and cut out, with a stand pasted on the back to support them.

If preferred, the walls may be covered with crayon or paint instead of wallpaper. If painted, the pieces should be weighted down at the corners while drying. If crayoned, color them after pasting on pictures, clocks, and the like, as paste does not stick very easily to waxed surfaces.

Goofy Goggles
By Frances Benson

Want to see someone turn purple or green? Just make a pair of goofy goggles. Draw the design on a small box or a piece of lightweight cardboard. Cut out the goggles and try them on for size. Cut them to fit over the nose just right, and to get the eyeholes big enough to see through easily.

Paint the frames with bright paints, making them really fancy. After the paint has dried, put in the colored "lenses," using colored cellophane from old Easter or Christmas wrappings. Tape a piece under each eyehole. Trim off the extra cellophane. Put on the goggles and look around. Everything and everybody will have a new color.

Crazy Faces
By Frances Benson

Here is an idea for unusual party decorations—make some crazy faces to tie around in various spots. Buy enough balloons so there is at least one for each guest, then paint faces on the balloons with fingernail enamel which dries quickly.

Use your imagination. Paint eyebrows, eyes, nose, mouth, sideburns, mustaches, beards, hair. Bits of cotton and cloth or corn silk can also be pasted on for hair.

When the guests leave, let each one select a balloon he likes, to take home. Perhaps some sort of contest could be arranged to determine just who gets the first choice, the second, and so on.

Mobiles By Barbara Baker

Cut a strip of yellow construction paper 12 inches long, 2 inches wide. Lap the ends and staple together to form a ring. Cut one edge into points as shown. Cut holes in opposite sides of the ring and insert string for a hanger.

Make chickens or birds from a square of colored construction paper folded in half to triangle shape. Punch a hole in the center of the fold and insert a string hanger with the knot inside the triangle. Slit the fold at both ends and insert paper tail feathers, comb, and bill, cut from constrasting colors. Staple or paste together. Cut feet and insert in the other point.

For objects like the eggs, cut two of each shape from contrasting colors and paste together with the string between.

The "snake" is cut from a circle of paper, starting at the outside edge and making one continuous circular cut to the center, or head. Eyes and tongue are from contrasting colors.

A hen, some baby chicks, and a coop make a good group; also favorite animals, birds, or fish.

Hang them from the circle at different levels.

A New Birthday Card
By Agnes Choate Wonson

Print letters and numbers in the squares as shown. Fill in the unused squares with different colors. At the bottom of the card, or on the back, print this rhyme:

Don't bother with definitions.
Just follow the numbers, they're few.
This crossword sends HAPPY BIRTHDAY, BEST WISHES FROM ME TO YOU!

Snowflakes By Ella L. Langenberg

Try cutting some delicate snowflake designs. Begin with a circle of thin paper. Fold as in Figures 1 to 3, then fold in half. Cut on solid line, Figure 4. This makes a six-sided figure.

Try other more complicated designs. Look for pictures of snowflakes. These will help in cutting good designs.

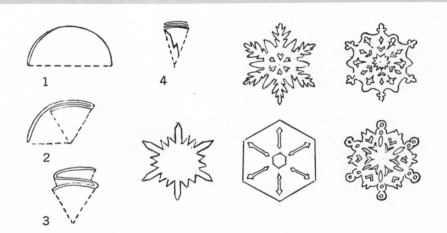

A New Use for Finger Painting
By Ruth Hunter

Materials needed are a square of glass, oilcloth with canvas backing, and finger paints.

Tape the edges of the glass to avoid cutting. Rub a damp sponge over the surface. Dab on bright-colored finger paint in several colors. Be careful not to smear the colors together or they will just blur.

With the fingertip or the side of the hand, make a design or outline a picture. The paint left after tracing through to the glass will become the picture.

Cut the oilcloth an inch larger than the glass. Press the canvas side over the painted glass, then gently peel it off. The design or picture will be stamped onto the oilcloth.

When the paint is dry, fold the edges of the oilcloth forward, and staple. This makes a shiny, colored frame for the picture.

Fun With Finger Paints
By Kathryn Staci

Fold a small sheet of paper in half, making a sharp crease. Open the paper and place a small dab of paint on the crease. Fold it again, smoothing it with the fingers until the paint is spread. Open the paper and try to guess what the picture resembles.

Then try putting two dabs of paint in the crease, each a different color.

A drop of ink from an old-style fountain pen can be used in the same way.

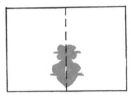 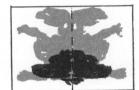

Spool Pictures By Bernice Walz

Find several empty spools of different sizes. Draw around one of the spools with a colored pencil or crayon. Add colored lines to make the face of a boy, girl, or clown.

Add a few lines here and there to some circles, to make a pair of glasses, a balloon, or some peas in a pod.

Try making some animals such as a turtle, mouse, or cat.

Finish the pictures by coloring them with paints or crayon.

Now try making some different and original pictures.

Homemade Finger Paint

By Shirley Hellner

Materials needed:
½ cup of lump starch
½ cup of cold water
1½ cups of boiling water
½ cup of white soap flakes
1 tablespoon of glycerin
fruit coloring

Dissolve the starch in the cold water. Add the hot water and cook the mixture until it is clear, stirring constantly. Add the soap flakes and stir. Remove from the stove immediately. When cool, stir in the glycerin, and enough coloring to give the desired shade.

Place Cards
By Barbara and Sue Baker

The girl and boy are made from wooden picnic spoons, with swab-stick arms and legs. Decorate them with water colors, ink, sequins, silver glitter, bits of cloth, ribbon, plastic, yarn, and the like. Set them in gumdrops, using a wire run through the girl's belt at the back, and a swab stick pasted to the boy's back. Print the guest's name on ribbon or paper attached to the doll.

The jet plane is made of painted popsicle sticks, cut, and held together with transparent gummed tape.

The illustrations are ideas to start from. Odds and ends on hand will suggest other decorations.

Fourth of July Cookies
By Carol Conner

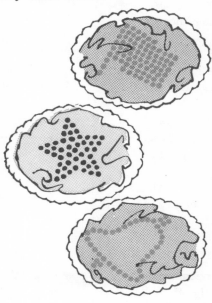

Spread frosting on top of butter crackers. Before it dries, add tiny candy cake decorations in silver, mixed colors, or plain colors like red, yellow, green, or chocolate.

To make the frosting, blend 2 tablespoons of melted butter or margarine into 1 cup of sifted powdered sugar. Add a small amount of milk, little by little, and ½ teaspoon of vanilla, until the frosting is thin enough to spread with a knife.

The decorations should be bright and gay. Dip some of the cookies, frosting side down, in a dish of multi-colored cake decorations. Make pictures on others using silver or colored decorations in the shape of a flag, for instance. Press the decorations lightly into the frosting so they will stay. What other pictures or designs would be fun to make on Fourth of July cookies?

Mosaic Tray
By Katherine Corliss Bartow

Enamel the underside of a cardboard meat tray in a solid color. Airplane gloss dope can also be used. Be sure to color the rim.

Cut colored squares and oblongs from greeting cards, or from plain-colored gift-wrap paper. Glossy-finished paper is best. Many colors can be used on the tray, or only two, such as red and black or pink and blue.

Work out the design before you start to glue. Cut the pieces to any size to make them fit. Glue them to the unpainted side of the tray with white glue. For added decoration on the mosaic design, cut flowers or figures from the color squares, or use a cutout of

a butterfly, deer, or other attractive subject from a greeting card. Cover the tray inside and out with a coat of shellac or clear fingernail polish.

This tray may be used for letters, pins, nuts and candy, or potted plants.

Nailhead Designs
By Virginia Appelt

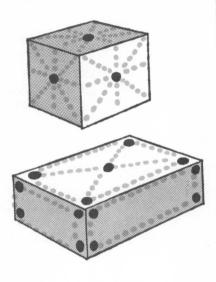

Blocks of wood decorated with nailhead designs make unusual articles such as doorstops, paperweights, book ends, and the like.

First, choose a block of wood the shape and size desired. Soft woods such as pine will be easiest to hammer nails into. Sandpaper the block until it is smooth and satiny, then stain or varnish it. A dark color will make the nailheads show up better. The wood may also be painted, though painting will hide the wood grain.

When dry, sketch a design lightly on the block with chalk, using straight lines, circles, stars, or initials. Then hammer in nails along the design lines. Use gold or silver-colored nails, or colored upholstery tacks for a brighter design. For variety, use nails with different-sized heads. The shorter the nails, the easier they will be to hammer in without splitting the wood. Put the nails fairly close together, and try to space them evenly.

Crayon Cut-and-paste Pictures
By Lois Marie Fink

Take crayons and paper, and go for a walk. Walk through the house. Go outside into the yard, too. Look all around for different kinds of surfaces — rough surfaces, smooth surfaces, crinkled surfaces — on such things as book covers, baskets, a wood floor, radiator, screen door, and the side of a tree. Place the paper on top of these different surfaces and rub the crayon against the paper. Remove the wrapping from the crayon and use the broad side, not the end.

Get five or six different crayon rubbings, then decide what will be in the picture — perhaps a house and yard, or animals at the zoo.

Cut out the shapes of these objects from the crayon rubbings. Arrange these cutouts on another piece of paper to make a picture. Then paste them down. Cut out more shapes from the crayon rubbings and put them in place to complete the picture. Cut strips of paper from the crayon rubbings and paste them around the outside of the picture as a frame.

rubbings

Uncle Sam
By Ruth E. Libbey

Use a pasteboard ribbon-spool for Uncle Sam's head. Paste a piece of white paper around the spool. With crayons or paint, draw eyes, nose, and mouth. Glue on a white cotton beard, hair, and eyebrows.

For the hatbrim cut a piece of red paper about a half inch wider than the top of the spool. Glue it to the top of the spool. Cut a strip of paper for the crown. Roll it into a tube and glue ends together. Cut little slits around both edges of the tube. Fold the tabs toward the center for gluing. Cut a small round piece of red paper, tracing around the crown for size. Glue it to the top of the crown, over the tabs. Glue the other end of the crown to the brim.

Color a red-white-and-blue hatband, and paste it around the hat.

Year Round

By Thelma T. Royer

Basket

Using the bottom part of the carton, cut off a section of four cups joined in one piece. This is the basket. For the handle, cut a strip from the lid of the carton, ½ inch wide and 10 inches long. Cut both ends to points.

Paint or color the handle. Use the same color on the outside of the basket, and a contrasting color on the inside. When both parts are dry, glue the handle to the basket or use a metal brad fastener. Fill the basket with candy or flowers.

Nut Cup

Use one egg section. Cut the top edge in points or wavy lines. Paint the inside a light color and the outside a darker color. The nut cup can also be used as a place card by pasting the bottom of the cup to a piece of heavy white paper, 2 by 4 inches.

Floating Candle

Use one egg section. Line the inside with aluminum foil, pressing out all wrinkles. Melt an old candle or piece of paraffin over low heat. Add bits of broken crayon to get the right color. Pour the melted wax into the egg carton. Fill about two-thirds of it. Before the wax gets hard, put a wick or piece of string in the center. When the wax is cool and hard, cut away the paper section and peel off the foil. This dainty little candle can be used in flower arrangements or as a decoration for a party.

Cowboy Hat

Use one egg section for the crown of the hat. Cut an oval-shaped brim from the carton lid. Place the crown in the center of the brim and trace around it. Punch a hole in the center of the circle and cut eight or ten slashes from center to circle. Glue these pointed ends to the inside of the crown. Paint the hat brown, tan, or black. Before the paint dries, roll up the brim so it looks like a real cowboy hat. Wrap a piece of string or yarn around the crown. Bring the ends through the holes punched in the brim. Tie together for a chin strap. To use as a place card, write the guest's name across the brim.

Let's Make a Dew Glass

By Marian Talmadge and Iris Gilmore

Materials: a pane of window glass, not too large, a basket of freshly gathered flowers, a small spade, and a big spoon.

Find a vacant spot in the garden, in the evening just at twilight. Dig a shallow hole a little smaller than the size of the window glass.

Arrange the flowers in the hole. Then, using the spoon, sprinkle them with water. Put the window glass over the hole so it is entirely covered.

Next morning, get up early before the sun reaches the garden. Hurry outside and look at the dew glass. There you will see a truly magic sight. There will be dewdrops trembling on the glass and all over the flowers.

Figure out different combinations of garden flowers, wild flowers, ferns, and branches. Try different kinds of arrangements. It is a wonderful surprise for friends and visitors who have never seen a dew glass.

78

A Window Screen Belt

By Thelma T. Royer

If the belt is to be a gold color, use copper screen. If silver is preferred, use aluminum screen. With ordinary kitchen scissors, cut a strip of screen 1½ inches wide and 1½ inches longer than the waist measurement desired. Trim off all excess bits of wire so the edges will be smooth to work with.

Cut two strips of bias tape as long as the belt. Open the tape and run glue along the top edge, the middle fold, and the lower edge. Press the tape over the edges of the screen to cover the raw sharp edges.

For the center trim, use colored ribbon or embroidered tape about

¾ inch wide. Cut a piece as long as the belt. Run glue along the back of it and press it firmly down the middle of the belt.

Cut two strips of edge trim the length of the belt. Glue it on top of the bias tape. This trim should be about ¼ inch wide, and should match the center trim in color or design. Use rickrack, lace, or any narrow trim that will cover the tape.

Fold back the screen belt ¾ inch on either end, and cover the rough edges with a strip of bias tape.

From the dime store buy a metallic buckle that resembles a giant hook and eye. Sew this buckle to the belt.

Bluebird Nut Cup

By Jinx Woolson

On 5½-by-8½ paper, make a pattern from the drawing shown. Fold it in half to cut, so both sides are alike. Lay it on heavy construction paper and cut around it, then cut the remaining solid lines. Fold in on the dotted lines.

Lap the ends to form the square cup, and paste. Fold the birds up to the sides of the cup and paste in place.

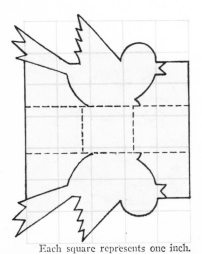

Each square represents one inch.

A Mask

By Barbara Baker

On a piece of board, arrange as features various "stick out" articles. Dip a piece of old muslin sheet in a solution of plaster of Paris. Lay it over the articles. Press and punch the muslin into the face shape desired. Let it dry for a day or so.

Leaving the articles under the mask, paint the entire face, then the features, with tempera paint. When dry, remove the mask. Bend any extra muslin edges to the back of the mask. Finish the face with a coat of shellac. Paste on hair made from yarn, string, or crepe paper. The mask will remain stiff.

Things To Do

Sea Monster
By Bonnie Leman

To make this fierce fellow, you will need an egg carton, two pipe cleaners, colored paper, paints or crayons, glue, and facial tissues.

Cut the egg carton into one row of six cups for the body, one row of two cups for the head, and three single cups for the neck and mouth.

Using the two pipe cleaners twisted together, thread it through the first cup of the body, then up through the two single cups for the neck, and then through one of the cups of the head. Stuff half a facial tissue up into each cup in the neck and head to keep them slightly separated. This will give the monster a neck that swivels.

For the mouth, cut the lower half off the remaining single cup. Push it up into the front half of the head. Glue in place.

Cut eyes and tongue from colored paper, and glue them on. Cut a slot in the end of the monster, and insert a tail cut from the lid of the egg carton. Paint the monster with poster paint, or color with crayons.

Shadow Box
By Ruth Hunter

This shadow box can be made from the cover of an egg carton or similar paper dish. Paint it with fall colors, and let it dry thoroughly.

Collect weeds of various shapes and sizes. Try them out against the background. An autumn leaf might add color and interest. When satisfied with the arrangement, fasten the weeds in place with a stapler or gummed tape.

Mr. Egghead With a Crewcut
By Rose Olson

Mr. Egghead is great fun to make and watch. From modeling clay, make a base for the empty eggshell to sit in. Fill the shell with dirt, and plant grass seed. Then paint a face, and stick on some ears cut from paper. In a few days Mr. Egghead will begin to grow hair which can be cut almost every day to keep him in a nice crewcut. Give the little man about two spoonfuls of water each day.

80

Jack-in-the-matchbox

By Virginia Appelt

Cut two strips of paper ½ to ¾ inch wide, and at least 10 to 11 inches long. Glue the end of one strip over the end of the other strip at right angles.

Fold one strip over the other at right angles, continuing to the end of the strips. Glue these ends together. This folded paper acts like a spring, popping up when it is released.

Draw, color, and cut out a funny face. Glue it to one end of the spring. Glue the other end of the spring to the inside bottom of a matchbox. Push the spring down, and close the matchbox. When the box is opened, Jack will pop up.

Aluminum Sailboat

By M. Mable Lunz

From an aluminum plate, such as frozen dinners come in, cut off one of the smaller corners for the bottom of the boat. Trim off the double edges along the outside.

From the large flat section of the plate, cut the sail, using the illustration for a guide.

Put two holes along the edge of the boat section. Twist the ends of the sail through these holes to hold it in place.

The boat will float on water.

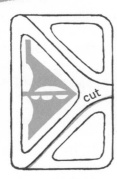

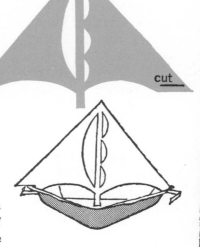

Powder-puff Fancies

By Agnes Choate Wonson

Tiny powder puffs, which are quite inexpensive, make unusual favors for gifts or parties. A head, a fish, and a flower are illustrated. Use gummed reinforcements for eyes and flower centers. Scraps of colored construction paper, make other decorations. Draw and cut out petals for the flower, fins and tail for the fish, ears and nose for the face. Paste these pieces in place.

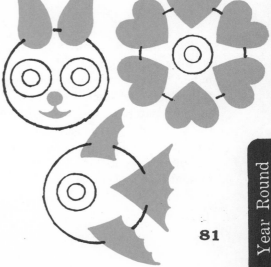

81

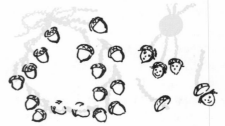

Plastic Bag Beanie
By Ida M. Pardue

Plastic bags, such as fruit, sweaters, and other products come in, make cute beanie hats.

Choose a bag big enough to fit the head. Tie a piece of colored yarn or gift-wrap ribbon around the bottom of the bag, about 2 inches up. This is the top of the hat. Turn the open end up once or twice in a wide cuff, until the hat is the right size. Decorate it with gummed seals or stars.

Butterflies
By Lillie D. Chaffin

To make a gay butterfly, fold a 3-by-6-inch piece of tissue paper, cellophane, or aluminum foil. Fasten a 2-inch pipe cleaner in the center with wire. Leave the two ends of the wire for the antenna. Stick a long pin through the center of the butterfly and into a pencil eraser. Blow on it, and it will whirl around.

Pencil Case
By M. Mable Lunz

Two pieces of imitation leather or plastic are needed, each 3 inches wide—one 11½ inches long, the other 7½ inches long. Two colors may be used.

Cut the ends of the pieces as shown. Cut two 1-inch slits in the small piece, ¼ inch apart, and 1½ inches down from the top.

Lay the small piece on the large one. Punch holes down each side, ½ inch apart. Space four holes evenly across the bottom. Make the holes with a paper punch, or place the material on a board, and hammer holes in it with a nail.

Cut a long narrow strip of the material. Lace it through the holes as shown. If the strip is not long enough, add another to it with household cement. Hold it with a paper clip until it dries. Cement the ends of the strip in place.

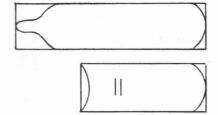

Acorn Jewelry
By Dorothy M. Clarke

For the lapel pin, choose three large perfect acorns. Remove the caps and pierce a hole through the center top of each. Cut a 6-inch length of green yarn for each cap. Knot the end and run it up through the hole. Glue the tops back onto the acorns. Cover each with nail polish, and paint on a face. Add some cloth or yarn for hair.

Cover a button with green felt or corduroy. Sew the yarn to the back of the button so the faces will dangle at different lengths, as shown. Sew a small safety pin to the back of the button.

An attractive necklace can be made by stringing these acorns on strands of gold thread or green yarn, then twisting the strands.

Novelty Pins
By Bernice Walz

Mix plaster of Paris and water together in a coffee can until it is like thick cream. Pour a little into the bottom of a crinkly baking cup. When it starts to harden, place a small open safety pin in the center. After the mixture is hard, peel off the paper cup. Paste a pretty colored picture of a child on the front of the pin. These can be cut from old greeting cards or magazines.

82

Soda-straw Boy

By Dorothy M. Clarke

This soda-straw boy can be made to walk and dance because he is jointed.

From a soda straw, cut four arm sections, each about 1½ inches long. Cut four leg sections about 2 inches long. Cut eight ½-inch sections for the vertebrae in the backbone.

Double a 36-inch piece of yarn and string on it the eight backbone pieces. Divide the yarn, and string two leg joints on each thread. Knot the yarn ends.

Tie a second piece of yarn at the neck, as shown. String on the arm sections. Tie a knot at each hand.

Cut two cardboard circles. Paint a boy's face on one of them. Paste the circles together with the top yarn loop between them.

Bottle Fun By Barbara Baker

All kinds of things can be made from empty bottles—people, animals, bugs, planes, creatures from another world, anything the shape of the bottle suggests.

Trim them with scraps of cloth, yarn, and other odds and ends. Fasten the trim to the bottle with glue or cellophane tape.

Doll Purse and Hat

By Margaret Grady

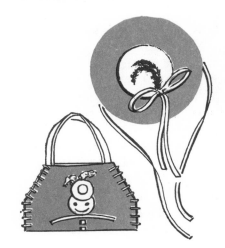

This doll hat and purse are made of contrasting colors of felt or other stiff material.

For the purse, cut out a piece 3 by 5 inches. Fold in half, cut off the corners, and stitch the sides together as shown, leaving the top open. Cut a strip of material for the handle about 5 inches long and ¼ inch wide. Sew it in place. The purse and handle can be of different colors.

For the doll-button decoration, glue a button to the side of the purse, the two holes being the eyes. The hat is two circles, one pasted over the other. The feather is a piece of yarn. The arms are a thin strip of material 1½ inches long. Two little dots of material make the buttons.

The doll hat is made from two circles of contrasting material, one 3½ inches in diameter, the other 1½ inches. Paste or sew the smaller circle to the center of the larger one. Make the bow from a 6-inch strip of material. Add a yarn feather. Fasten a strip of material to the underside of the hat, long enough to tie in a bow under the doll's chin.

Bicycle Name Plate

By M. Mable Lunz

Use scrap wood ¼ or ⅜ inch thick. Cut a piece 3 by 5 inches. Smooth the edges and surface with sandpaper. Paint it white, and let it dry. If necessary, give it a second coat.

Cut ¼-inch strips from red light-reflecting bumper tape. Put a strip of the tape all around the edge, and nickname or initials in the center. Use several straight pieces of tape for each letter. Make them about 2 inches high. Bright paint may be used instead of bumper tape, if preferred.

Drill holes through the top of the plate, and wire it to the back of the bike.

Upside-down Man

By Gertrude Schlesinger

This man is smiling, but turn him upside down and he cries.

Make other upside-down people. Be sure the eyes and ears are at about the center of the head. Try out the rest of the lines in pencil, then go over them with ink or crayon.

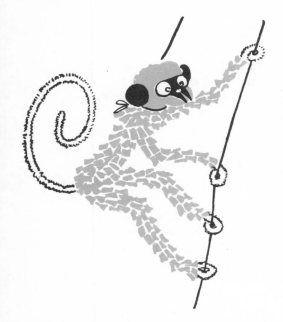

Tiny Spider Monkey   By Betty Merritt

Cut a pipe cleaner in half. Use one piece for the arms, the other for the legs, bending at the center and curling the ends for hands and feet.

Bend another pipe cleaner in half. Attach the legs at the bend, giving them an extra twist to hold them in place. Attach the arms in the same way, about ¾ inch from the legs. Coil the pipe cleaner end into a head shape. Bend and coil the opposite end into a tail.

Cut face and ears from colored paper, the eyes from white. Paste to the head shape.

For fur, cut a long strip of colored crepe paper about 1 inch wide. Fold it in half the long way, cut slits in the folded edge about ⅛ inch apart, and wind the strip around the pipe cleaner.

To make the monkey climb, tie one end of a long string around his neck. Run the other end through his hands and feet. Place the loop over a finger, pull on the string, and he will climb.

Make a Glamorous Wastebasket

By Rebecca Roman

A large-sized oatmeal box, covered with plain wallpaper, may be made into a good-looking wastebasket.

Before pasting the paper to the box, decorate it with a picture of a pet cat or dog, or a favorite animal or bird. The diagrams show an easy way to make a pattern of an owl or cat by drawing half of the figure on a fold of paper, then cutting it out. Trace around it on the wallpaper, then fill in the rest of the picture, using heavy crayon lines.

After the wallpaper is firmly pasted to the box, add sequins or dime-store jewels for eyes, claws, and other decorative touches. Special glue for the jewels may be bought at the dime store.

Candle Sculpture

By Yvonne A. Bildahl

Here is a worth-while use for old candles. With a penknife, round the top of the candle to represent the head. Leave the wick, which can be frayed to look like hair.

Cut two notches for the eyes. Turn the candle sideways, and carve the profile. Cut away part of the cheeks to form the nose. Carve the lips, teeth, and mouth. Shape the cheeks by carving away sides of the candle.

Smooth the entire carving by scraping lightly with knife blade. If desired, the face can be painted —blue eyes, red cheeks and lips, and a collar if one has been carved.

Try making a totem pole or other objects that can be carved from a candle.

Whatizzit

By Barbara Baker

Cut several different shapes from newspaper or colored construction paper. Turn them round and round until one of them looks like something—perhaps a funny animal, an island, a face, a monster.

Paste the shape to a large piece of colored paper. Then try to make it really look like the object it resembles by adding scraps of colored paper. Try to give it a 3-D look by pasting only one end of a strip, letting the other end go free to fold, curl, or fringe.

Felt Coin Purse

By Louise Ewing

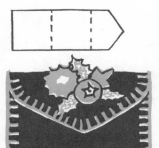

Cut a strip of dark-colored felt, tapering it at one end to form the flap, as shown. Fold like an envelope. With bright yarn, decorate the flap. Fasten the sides with a blanket stitch. Start at the lower left corner, go up the side, around the edge of the flap, and down the right side. Cut out bright felt flowers and green leaves, and sew to the flap. Sew a snap on the underside to fasten the flap down.

Plastic Bag and Ribbon Belt

By M. Mable Lunz

Many vegetables are now sold in small plastic bags with pretty printed tops. Cut off the tops of two plastic bags, about 4 inches down. Cut a piece of ribbon about 10 inches long. Slide the two plastic loops over the ribbon. Sew the ribbon ends together.

Slide another piece of ribbon through one of the plastic loops. Put the belt around the waistline. Slide the ribbon through the plastic loop on the other side, pull up the ribbon to fit, and tie a bow in the front. Cut off the ribbon ends to the desired length.

Bandana Apron

By Bernice Walz

This apron is good-looking, and easy to make.

Use a bandana handkerchief 2 feet square. Fold over 9 inches at the top to make a tiered effect. Stitch across it 1 inch down from the fold, to make a heading. Cut a ¾-inch ribbon, 1½ yards long. Pull it through the heading and gather. Allow about 20 inches of ribbon on either side for ties, then stitch at both ends of the heading to hold the gathers in place.

Puppet Show

By Barbara Baker

The Stage

Make the stage from a large cardboard carton. Cut off the top. Cut a large square hole in one side as shown. This is the front of the stage which will face the audience. Leave a frame around the hole wide enough so the puppets may be let down onto the sides of the stage as they appear, without being seen by the audience.

The background scenery goes inside the box, opposite the big hole. Paint the scenery on large sheets of paper, a little smaller than the backside of the stage. Make one for each scene in the play, print the title of the play on another sheet, and "The End" on another. Lay them one under the other in the proper order. Fasten them together with masking tape into one long strip.

Cut a broom handle in half to make two rollers. Attach one to each end of the scenery strip. The strip may then be rolled off one handle onto the other, as the scenery is changed.

Cut holes in the sides of the stage box and insert the rollers as shown. Let the ends stick out for easy turning. Place the holes so the scenery will cover as much of the stage back as possible without crowding the rolls.

Cover the rest of the box, inside and out, with bright-colored paint or paper. Fasten cloth curtains to the front of the box, with a cord through the top hem so they may be pulled apart when the play starts.

Puppet shows are most effective in a darkened room so the

puppet operators cannot be seen. The stage may be lighted with a flashlight held by a member of the audience, or Christmas tree lights can be placed inside the front of the box for footlights.

The stage should be placed on a table where it can be seen comfortably by the audience.

The Puppets

For the puppet's head, crush a ball of tissue, cover it with a larger tissue, and tie at the neck. Divide the ends of the tissue into legs and tie them apart. Make arms from another tissue, rolled up and secured to the neck by string. Tie them at the wrists, leaving an end of string from each wrist long enough to let the puppet down onto the stage. If the head falls over, pin a long string to the top so the operator can hold it up.

Use paint or felt for the face and clothes. Make one puppet for each character in the play. Animals will need one string attached to the top of the head and another to the tail end of the body.

The Play

Records may be played and the action pantomimed with the puppets. Or favorite stories may be acted out by the puppets, with one person reading the story part, and a different person for each character as it speaks. And it's fun for a group to make up a play and "read" their own parts.

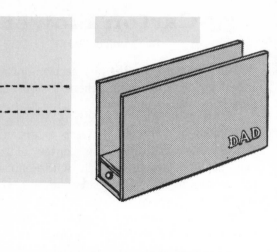

A Letter Holder for Father

By Virginia Follis

Cut a piece of cardboard about 6 by 9¾ inches. Fold it across the 6-inch width as shown, so that matchboxes will fit in the center fold. The center strip will probably be about 1½ inches wide. Cut a strip of cardboard 1½ by 6 inches. This will be pasted over the top of the matchboxes later.

Cover the larger piece of cardboard with wallpaper, or colored construction paper, using library paste or wheat paste. Be sure to fold and paste the paper carefully around the folds of the cardboard so the paper will not split as it dries.

When dry, paste or glue the matchboxes in place in the center strip, using household cement. Space the boxes so the edge of each is in line with the outside of the cardboard, as shown. These boxes will be drawers to hold paper clips and stamps. Punch a hole in the end of the drawer of each matchbox. Decorate the end of the box to match the letter holder. Insert paper fasteners in the holes for drawer pulls.

Cover the small strip of cardboard to match the letter holder. Paste or glue it over the matchboxes. Put plenty of paste on the sides of the matchboxes. Fold up the sides of the letter holder and press them against the boxes. Carefully place two rubber bands or some string around the letter holder until the boxes have dried thoroughly.

If plain paper has been used, add Dad's name as a decoration.

A Snowstorm Paperweight

By Frances Benson

Find a small round jar (like a jelly jar) with a tight-fitting cap. Clean it thoroughly. Pour hot melted paraffin into the jar cap. Set a small plastic ornament, that will fit in a winter scene, into the paraffin and let it harden. Fill the jar with water and add fine-ground moth flakes. Screw the cap (with the ornament attached) on tight, turn the jar upside down, and give it a shake.

A Monogrammed Bookmark

By Rebecca Roman

Make a pattern for the bookmark by using a thin piece of cardboard about 3 inches by 5 inches. Fold the cardboard lengthwise so that both sides of the design may be cut at the same time. See the diagram for cutting instructions.

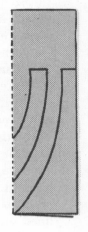

Using this pattern, cut the bookmark from another piece of cardboard. Use ink, water colors, or crayons for Dad's monogram and the design.

Baskets From Boxes
By Virginia Follis

Collect pieces of corrugated cardboard, or ask a grocer for any kind of interesting packing material which he usually throws away, such as the bumpy paper used for liners in large egg cartons.

Cut a cereal box or cake-mix box as shown. Fasten the side ends together to form a handle. Cut and paste the bumpy paper or the corrugated cardboard to the box sides, or fasten it on with paper fasteners, two on each side. Paint it with thick water colors or tempera paint, using two coats if necessary.

The egg liners have different kinds of designs which can be painted as desired. Corrugated paper can be decorated with cutouts. Cover the rest of the box and the handle with paint or colored construction paper.

Corrugated paper from cooky packages may be used if desired. It is usually colored and needs no painting. Dry soup envelopes are lined with pretty aluminum paper which can be cut into designs and pasted on the basket. Many other trimmings can be used from packages in the kitchen.

These baskets make lovely gifts when filled with candy or flowers. Decorate with a bow of ribbon if desired.

Egg-Carton Flowers
By Bernice Walz

Cut out and trim the cup sections of a cardboard egg carton. Paint them inside and outside with water colors.

Bouquet or Corsage. Insert a green pipe-cleaner stem through the center bottom of each section, letting ¼ inch of the end extend up inside the cup. Over this end, slip a round white or yellow circle cut from a lace-paper doily, to form the flower center. Paste green construction paper leaves on the stem.

Make several of these flowers. Trim the stems to various lengths and put the flowers into a small vase for a bouquet. Or tie a cluster of flowers together with ribbon to make a corsage.

Flower Cluster. Make each flower as before, but fold over the ¼-inch end of the stem to hold securely. Use a bit of the curly material from a metal pot scraper for the flower center, fastening it to the folded end with rubber cement.

Make two or more such flowers. Cut the stems somewhat shorter and twist them on either side of a long pipe-cleaner stem. Paste green construction paper leaves on the stem.

Water Lily. Make the lily as for the flower cluster. Paste it with rubber cement to the center of a green construction paper leaf which has been cut to represent a water lily pad. If the lily pad is cut from a section of a green waxed-paper cup, the flower will float on water like a real water lily.

How To Model Animals and Birds With Clay

By Kay H. Persing

Materials needed:

A can of self-hardening moist clay.
A wooden board, such as a breadboard.
A half yard of oilcloth, placed rough side up on the board.
A modeling tool or orange stick from the dime store.
A sponge to keep fingers free from clay.
A plastic bag to keep the clay model from getting dry until it is finished.

Any animal or bird may be modeled with clay by following the instructions given. First read the instructions. Then, before beginning to model, try rolling the clay for a little while, to get the feel of it, and to learn to handle it with confidence. This will also remove the air bubbles and make the clay firm.

Take enough clay from the can to form a ball the size of an orange or a tennis ball. Roll it round and round in the hands to remove air bubbles. Place it on the board. Roll it back and forth to form a cylinder about 6 inches long and 1 inch in diameter.

Cut the cylinder in six pieces as illustrated. Section 1 will form the head, and 2 will form the body. Sections 3, 4, 5, and 6 will be the four legs of an animal, or two legs and two wings of a bird.

Take more clay from the can and roll a ball about the size of a marble. Press it flat with the thumb. Cut out two pear-shaped pieces for the ears. Make a tiny roll for the tail, and a little ball for the nose. For fur, roll tiny cylinders of clay and coil them. Moisten and attach to body.

Before pressing the different parts in place, each piece should be roughened with the modeling tool and dampened.

All animals and birds are egg-shaped. Learn to form perfect little egg-shaped pieces—small for the head, larger for the body, and little pieces to connect, such as the neck. Keep this egg form in mind, and it will be very easy to model a pet dog, horse, rabbit, or bird.

head   body   leg   leg

leg   leg

89

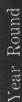

Animal Pop Ups

By Marjorie Weed

All the creatures on this page are made by starting with a pear-shaped piece of paper from 5 to 8 inches long, cut on the fold as shown. A slit is cut in each end so that ends may be folded to bring the desired shape. After cutting the pear-shaped piece for the body, cut the other pieces the right size to fit. Look at the suggestions for each creature.

Make other animals, starting with the pear-shaped piece of paper.

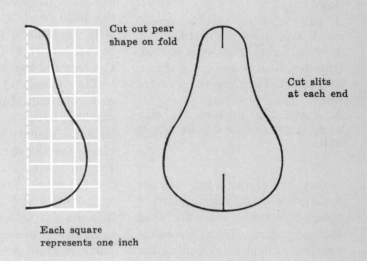

Cut out pear shape on fold

Cut slits at each end

Each square represents one inch

Bunny Head

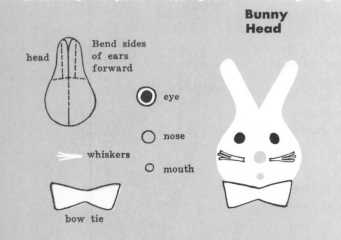

head

Bend sides of ears forward

eye

nose

whiskers

mouth

bow tie

Skunk

mouth

eye

ear

body

back stripe

tail stripe

tail

Whale

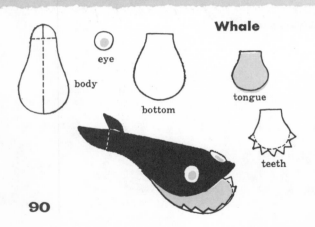

eye

body

bottom

tongue

teeth

Rabbit

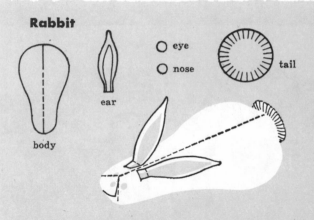

body

ear

eye

nose

tail

Let's Have Fun With Chalk

By Evelyn White Minshull

Chalk and potatoes. Doesn't sound very appetizing, does it? Not a bit like mashed potatoes with rich brown gravy, or baked potatoes with butter, or crisp french fries. Well, you're not supposed to EAT it.

Perhaps you never thought of potatoes as a means of expressing yourself through art. With simple forms, you can create anything from flowers to fences, borders to butterflies, and all sorts of other things!

All you need is a cup partly full of water, a paring knife, colored chalk and, of course, a potato.

Instead of planning your entire design, think in small units. When you begin to print, lots of ideas will come to you as to how these units might be used. Think first of simple shapes, Figure 1. Add a few slender ones for variety, Figure 2. Then modify simple shapes, Figure 3.

Don't bother to peel the potato. If the peeling remains on the back or even the side of your printing piece, it won't hurt a thing.

Leave the printing pieces fairly thick, as shown in Figure 4, so that you can hold them comfortably.

To print, dip the desired color of chalk into the water, then smear over the printing area of the potato. Press the potato firmly to the paper. Sometimes several prints may be made before putting more chalk on the potato. Different types of paper will produce varied effects. Experiment until you find the effect you consider most striking.

Don't expect the printing to be perfect. There will be places where the color gathered, places where it is extremely thin — even where it failed to print at all. Don't try to change it. This is one of the charms of potato-chalk art. Each design is distinctive and individual. Keep experimenting.

Figure 5 illustrates similar flowers with different types of foliage. Can you think of several other leaf shapes which might have been used? And different ways in which the leaves might have been placed? (By the way, the stem was printed with the edge of a very slim piece.)

Why not try a bunch of grapes? A tree with autumn foliage? A bed of tulips? Birds?

Try all of these and more, and you'll find that potatoes produce beauty for the eyes as well as enjoyment for the tummy. Just remember the recipe: potatoes and chalk.

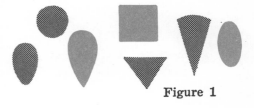

Figure 1

Figure 2

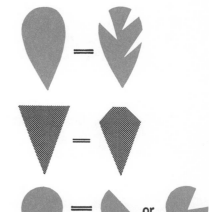

Figure 3

Figure 4

Figure 5

91

Doll Hat Party Favors
By Nora Diltz

For the brim of the hat, cut a 4-inch circle or oval from stiff colored paper. Trim the hat with a bunch of flowers, or a little bouquet of paper ribbon, tying it to the crown with narrow silk or paper ribbon. Bring the ribbon ends through the crown and tie in a large bow on the underside. Cut a hole in the brim for a crown, and push a small nut cup through it.

Woven Purse   By Velma Colvin

To make this purse you need a skein of cotton rug yarn, a large needle, and straight pins.

Cut a piece of cardboard carton 5 by 7 inches. In one of the 5-inch ends, push straight pins, about ¼ inch apart. Let ¼ inch of each pin extend above the edge of the cardboard. There must be an odd number of pins. This will be the top of the purse.

Push one pin, at an angle, in the bottom right-hand corner as shown. Place the end of the rug yarn securely under the head of this pin. Bring the yarn to the top and around the first pin, then back down the same side, under the cardboard, and up the other side, and around the second pin. Continue this until the cardboard is strung with yarn to the last pin. Tie the yarn to the last pin with a single knot and leave about 36 inches of yarn loose.

Thread the end of this loose piece of yarn into a large needle, and begin weaving. Always weave with a single thread. With the needle go under the first thread, over the next, and so on, around and around the cardboard. Keep the weaving pushed up close to the last row so the weaving will be firm and strong.

Weave about twelve rows around, then drop down about ½ inch with your next row of weaving. This leaves a space in which to put the string handles of the purse.

When the weaver thread becomes short, tie another 36-inch piece of yarn to it and continue.

Continue the weaving around the cardboard to the bottom, keeping each row pushed up close. Tie the weaving thread in a secure knot to one of the threads at the bottom, and cut off.

Remove the pins, and slip the purse off the cardboard, working gently. Then turn the purse inside out. Where new pieces of thread were added, bring all knots to the inside.

Now cut six pieces of yarn, each 24 inches long. Use three pieces for each handle, knotting at one end and braiding together. Fasten a safety pin through the knot of one handle. Beginning at one side of the purse in the ½-inch open space, go under and over each thread all the way around the purse, coming out with the handle at the place you started. Remove the safety pin, untie the knot, then tie both ends of the handle together.

Do the same with the second handle, starting on the opposite side of purse. Cut the tied ends even.

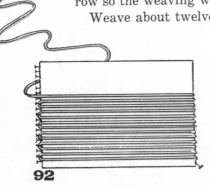
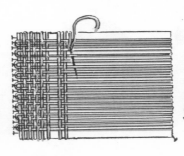
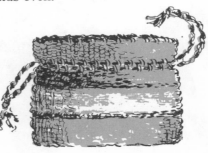

Scratch Pictures

By Virginia Appelt

To make these pictures, use old post cards or heavy manila envelopes or file folders.

Cover one side of the paper with bands or blotches of color, using bright crayons. When the paper is covered, go over it again, using a black crayon. Apply the black heavily to hide the colors completely.

To "scratch" the design or picture, use something like a bobby pin or a pointed stick. Try different kinds of scratchers for different results. It is fascinating to watch the bright colors pop out as the black is scratched away. Don't scratch too hard or the color underneath may scratch away, too.

Polish the finished picture with a paper handkerchief to give it a soft gleam.

Toothpick Pictures

By Jean T. Harris

Make toothpick pictures on a sheet of white or manila paper. Arrange the design on the paper with whole or broken toothpicks, then glue them in place. Fill in the remainder of the picture with colored crayons. Colored toothpicks may also be used.

Twist a String and Make Something

By M. Mable Lunz

To make a belt, cut eight pieces of yarn 2½ yards long. Put them together with the ends even. One person holds one end, another person the other end, standing far enough apart so the yarn is tight. One person twists the yarn in one direction, the other person twists it in the opposite direction.

When the yarn is very tight, fold it in half. One person then takes both the ends and holds them fast while the other person twists gently from the center. Then let the center go and the cord will twist itself completely. Before letting go, tie a knot about three inches up from the open end. Then tie a knot three inches up from the other end. Cut off both ends evenly, and the belt is ready to wear.

All cords are made in the same way. When starting, always cut the pieces of string two-and-a-half times as long as the finished length desired. Always be sure to tie a knot in the open end before letting go. Cords may be made in long lengths, then cut into shorter pieces—but be sure to tie knots before cutting them.

By using different colors, textures, and sizes of string, yarn, or crochet cotton, these cords may be made for any number of uses —bows for trimming petticoats, lamp shades, gift packages—ties for baby clothes, doll clothes, curtain tiebacks—cords for cowboy hats, light pulls, picture hangers.

Popcorn Jewelry   By Bernice Walz

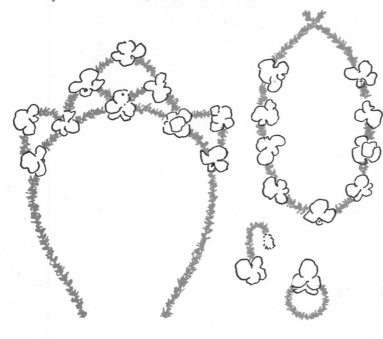

Try these ideas, then try some original designs.

RING. Cut a 3-inch piece of colored pipe cleaner. Attach a piece of popcorn in the center with rubber cement. Let it set till dry. Twist the ends together to fit the finger.

EARRINGS. Cut two 2-inch pieces of pipe cleaner. Paste a piece of popcorn on one end of each piece. When dry, paste a bit of cotton on the other two ends to cover the wire. Bend them to fit the ears.

BRACELET. Twist together two 6-inch lengths of pipe cleaner. Paste popcorn kernels about a half inch apart along them. Leave about two inches free at the ends. Twist them together to fit the wrist.

NECKLACE. Twist the ends of three 6-inch lengths of pipe cleaner together. Finish like the bracelet.

CROWN. Twist the ends of several pipe cleaners together to make a piece to fit around the head. Make loops of pipe cleaners across the front to fashion a crown. Paste popcorn here and there for jewels.

Candy Cups   By Lillie D. Chaffin

Attractive individual candy cups can easily be made from bright-colored cotton material. Cut a 4-inch circle of cloth for each cup. Pink the edge as shown. Dip the circle into heavy starch or paraffin and shape it over the bottom of a jelly glass or similar shape. Hold it in place with a rubber band until the wax dries.

A set of six will make a nice gift. Stack them together, place in a small plastic bag, and tie with a bright ribbon.

Name Cutouts   By Elizabeth Paris

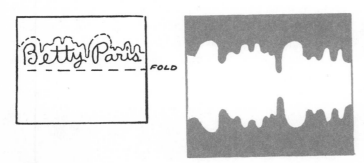

Select two sheets of colored construction paper, one dark and one light. Fold one of the sheets in half, lengthwise. Along the folded edge write a name in big, bold letters. Go around the tops of the letters again to make a good outline. Cut carefully around the tops of the letters. Unfold the cutout and paste it on the other paper.

Do some friends' names in the same way and see if they can guess the names. These make wonderful designs and look well on the wall.

Fish and Boat

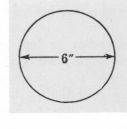

By Martha Carpenter

For the fish, cut a 6-inch circle from light-colored cardboard. Trace around it on plain paper and add the tail and lines to make a pattern. Lay the pattern with the edge of the tail on a fold of black construction paper and cut around it. Unfold. Cut out the design along the heavy lines on one circle. Then cut the second circle to match. Insert the colored circle. Paste together at the circle edges only. Cut a mouth shape from the colored circle edge. Paste a colored felt eye on each side. Add a black thread hanger. Bend out the black cutout sections.

For the boat, make the three patterns shown. Cut the boat with the bottom on a fold of gilt paper, and the two sails from lightweight white cardboard. Insert two balsa sticks between the folded boat sections as illustrated. Paste together. Paste the sails to the mast, one at the back, one in front. Tie white thread from bowsprit to mast, leaving a long end for a hanger.

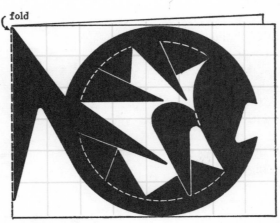

Each square represents one inch

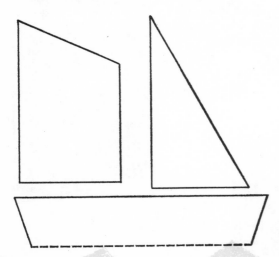

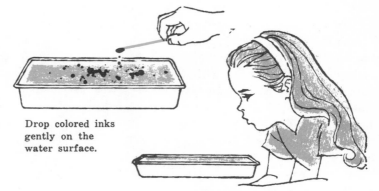

Water Printing

By Barbara Thieman

To make marbleized paper, fill a shallow pan with about one inch of water. Drop India ink colors gently on top, using a small brush or cotton swab stick. Only the colors that float on top of the water will make the design, so do not pour the ink in. Start with black ink. It helps outline and intensify the other colors.

Create a motion in the water by blowing the water or by gently moving the fingers through it. Then place the paper on top of the inked surface and allow it to remain in that position for ten seconds. Remove the paper and allow it to dry flat, design side up. Move the water surface each time, before placing the next paper, so that no two designs are exactly alike.

Now let's find ways to use these designs.

Turn them around in various directions and find pictures in them. Tell a story about the various objects found in each design.

Another use for these prints is to make them into a scrapbook cover. Fold a piece of cardboard or heavy drawing paper in half. When folded, it should be an inch smaller all around than the water prints. Paste a print on each side of the fold. Fold over the extra edges, top and bottom, to the inside of the cover, and paste. Trim the corners and paste. Paste another print, or some colored paper across the entire inside surface to finish. Cover the middle crease on the outside with a heavy, wide tape.

Or make a wastepaper basket, using a round oatmeal or ice-cream container. Use tape to reinforce the top edge and the bottom of the container. Line the inside with colored paper or paint it a bright color. Paste a water print around the outside, using plenty of paste on the overlapping edges.

Drop colored inks gently on the water surface.

Blow lightly to mix the inks.

Outline shapes with black or colored crayon.

Use marbleized paper to decorate scrapbook cover or wastebasket.